Historic Coupar Angus

the archaeological implications of development

E Patricia **Dennison**

Russel **Coleman**

the Scottish burgh survey

in association with

SCOTTISH CULTURAL PRESS

CENTRE FOR SCOTTISH URBAN HISTORY
Department of Scottish History
University of Edinburgh

PERTH & KINROSS COUNCIL

PERTH AND KINROSS HERITAGE TRUST

publication	Historic Scotland *in association with* Scottish Cultural Press First published 1997

editorial	Olwyn Owen
design	Christina Unwin
printing . binding	British Printing Company, Aberdeen
ISSN	1358 0272
Scottish Cultural Press ISBN	1 898218 48 X
all distribution **and sales enquiries** Scottish burgh survey	Scottish Cultural Press Unit 14 . Leith Walk Business Centre 130 Leith Walk Edinburgh EH6 5DT telephone *0131* 555 5950 . facsimile *0131* 555 5018
all other enquiries	▪ Scottish burgh surveys Centre for Scottish Urban History Department of Scottish History University of Edinburgh EH8 9LN telephone *0131* 650 4032 . facsimile *0131* 650 4032 ▪ Historic Scotland Longmore House Salisbury Place Edinburgh EH9 1SH telephone *0131* 668 8600 . facsimile *0131* 668 8699
British Library cataloguing **in publication data**	A catalogue record for this book is available from the British Library

contents

figures

APS	*The Acts of the Parliaments of Scotland*, ed Thomson & Innes (Edinburgh, 1814–75).
Charters	*Charters of the Abbey of Coupar Angus*, ed Easson, 2 vols (SHS, 1947).
Cowan & Easson	*Medieval Religious Houses. Scotland*, edd Cowan & Easson (London, 1976).
CSP Scot	*Calendar of State Papers Relating to Scotland and Mary Queen of Scots*, 13 vols, edd J Bain *et al* (Edinburgh, 1898–1969).
DES	*Discovery and Excavation in Scotland.*
NMRS	National Monuments Record of Scotland.
NRAS	National Register of Archives (Scotland).
NSA	*The New Statistical Account of Scotland* (Edinburgh, 1845).
OSA	*The Statistical Account of Scotland, 1791–1799*, ed Sir John Sinclair. New Edition, edd Grant & Withrington (Wakefield, 1973).
PSAS	*Proceedings of the Society of Antiquaries of Scotland.*
RCAHMS	Royal Commission on the Ancient and Historical Monuments of Scotland.
Rental	*Rental Book of the Cistercian Abbey of Cupar-Angus, with the Breviary of the Register*, ed Rogers, 2 vols (Grampian Club, 1879–80).
RMS	*The Register of the Great Seal of Scotland*, edd Thomson *et al* (Edinburgh, 1882–1914).
RPC	*The Register of the Privy Council of Scotland*, edd Burton *et al* (Edinburgh, 1877–).
RRS	*Regesta Regum Scottorum 1153–1406*, edd Barrow *et al* (Edinburgh, 1960–).
RSS	*Register of the Privy Seal of Scotland (Registrum Secreti Sigilli Regum Scotorum)*, edd Livingstone *et al* (Edinburgh, 1908).
SBRS	Scottish Burgh Records Society.
SHS	Scottish History Society.
SRO	Scottish Record Office, Edinburgh.
SUAT	Scottish Urban Archaeological Trust.
TA	*Accounts of the Lord High Treasurer of Scotland*, edd Dickson *et al* (Edinburgh, 1877–).

acknowledgements

The Centre for Scottish Urban History is indebted to a number of people for their assistance and advice.

Especial thanks go to the many local people who offered us advice, guided tours of the town and the loan of photographs and articles of interest, so giving us important insights into historic Coupar Angus. We would like to mention, in particular, Mrs Margaret Laing of Moorfields, Bendochy for the time and assistance she gave us. Mrs Jo Kettles, Mrs Sheila Forsyth, Mrs Morag Croall and Mr Jim Pitkeathly also willingly shared their local knowledge. Our only regret is that we did not have time to avail ourselves fully of all they had to offer. The help of Mr and Mrs Robson of the Royal Hotel, Mr Joseph Richards, Mr Christopher Dingwall of Ardler and the staff of Wm Culross and Son Ltd, was invaluable in tracking down old photographs and illustrations of the town.

We would also like to mention the staff at the **Town Hall, Coupar Angus**; Mrs L Mitchell and Mr J Duncan of **A K Bell Library, Perth**; Mr Mark Hall of **Perth and District Museum**; and Ms Rachael Tilling of the **Planning Department, (then) Perth and Kinross District Council** for their assistance. We have also benefited from discussions with Professor G W S Barrow, Edinburgh.

The Royal Commission on the Ancient and Historical Monuments of Scotland has been particularly supportive as has staff of **Historic Scotland**, in particular Ms Deirdre Cameron. The staff of the **Scottish Record Office** and of the **National Library of Scotland**, at both George IV Bridge and the Map Library at Causewayside, have been very helpful. Editorial assistance has been provided by Ms V J McLellan and Mrs Melissa Seddon. The index has been prepared by Mrs Hilary Flenley. The illustrations were collated by Mr Robin Macpherson.

For permission to reproduce photographs and illustrations, we wish to thank the following:

figures 3 *&* **4** are reproduced by kind permission of **The Secretary of State for Scotland**. © Crown Copyright.

figures 5, **7**, **8** *&* **10** are reproduced by kind permission of the **Royal Commission on the Ancient and Historical Monuments of Scotland**. © Crown Copyright: RCAHMS.

figure 6 is reproduced by kind permission of **Historic Scotland**. © Crown Copyright.

figures 9, **18**, **21** *&* **25** are reproduced by kind permission of the **Trustees of the National Library of Scotland**.

figure 11 is reproduced by kind permission of **Dr Pat Dennison**, Centre for Scottish Urban History, University of Edinburgh.

figures 12 *&* **24** are reproduced by kind permission of **Mr & Mrs A Robson**, Royal Hotel, Coupar Angus.

figures 13, **15**, **20** *&* **23** are reproduced by kind permission of **Mr Joseph Richards**, Coupar Angus.

figure 14 is reproduced by kind permission of **Mrs Margaret Laing**, Coupar Angus.

figure 22 is reproduced by kind permission of **Perth Museum and Art Gallery** (photograph by Mr John Watt, Almondbank, Perth).

figures 1, **2**, **16**, **17**, **19** *&* **26** are based upon the Ordnance Survey 1:10,000 scale and the Ordnance Survey 1:2,500 map series, with the permission of **The Controller of Her Majesty's Stationery Office**. © Crown Copyright, Licence number GD03032G/1997.

foreword

Settlement at Coupar Angus may date to at least the reign of David I (1124–53), but its development depended upon the Cistercian monastery founded on land allocated by Malcolm IV (1156–65) in 1159. The monastery received many gifts, and became an extensive establishment that attracted a lay settlement of workers and craftsmen—and a weekly market—to its gate. The Reformation caused serious disputes over the rights to Coupar Angus, but the matter was resolved in 1607 when Coupar Angus became a burgh of barony. The construction of a tolbooth and the creation of burgesses followed, and the population increased. The further prosperity of the town was linked to its market, and later to the growth of the linen industry in the eighteenth century. *Historic Coupar Angus* explores the town's history and development from its origins up to the nineteenth century, and examines its twin influences of religion and trade. Building on this information, the survey assesses what archaeological evidence of the burgh's historic past might survive beneath the streets, buildings and open spaces of present-day Coupar Angus.

Historic Coupar Angus is one of a series of reports on the historic burghs of Scotland—known collectively as the *Scottish Burgh Survey*—all of which have been commissioned by **Historic Scotland** and its predecessors. The main aim of the survey is to identify those areas of the present and historic burgh which are of archaeological interest and therefore require sensitive treatment in the event of any proposed development or other ground disturbance. It is designed primarily as a manual for the use of local authorities and archaeological curators. As an essential prerequisite, however, to this assessment of the archaeological implications of development, it also describes and illustrates the geography and topography of the town, its known archaeology and history, its historic standing buildings and the origins of its street names—all of which will be of interest to the wider public, be they inhabitant, visitor or student.

Historic Coupar Angus was prepared for Historic Scotland within **the Centre for Scottish Urban History**, under the supervision of its Director, Dr E Patricia Dennison. The Centre is part of the Department of Scottish History, University of Edinburgh. Dr Dennison and Mr Russel Coleman, of the **Scottish Urban Archaeological Trust**, are co-authors of the report; Mr Kevin Hicks, of the **Centre for Field Archaeology**, University of Edinburgh, is cartographer and illustrator. Dr Alan MacDonald and Mr Robin Macpherson of the Scottish History Department acted as Research Assistants; and assistance was also received from Ms Sharon Adams, Mr Jim McCormack and Ms Ruth Grant, all postgraduates in the Department of Scottish History, and Mr Simon Stronach from SUAT. The project is supervised by the Head of the Department, Professor Michael Lynch, and managed for Historic Scotland by Ms Olwyn Owen, Inspector of Ancient Monuments, who is also general editor of the series.

The research on historic Coupar Angus was carried out during August and September 1995. This survey was entirely funded by Historic Scotland with help from the Centre for Scottish Urban History. The report has been published with financial assistance from **Perth and Kinross Council**, **Perth and Kinross Heritage Trust** and Historic Scotland. Further copies may be obtained from **Scottish Cultural Press**, Unit 14, Leith Walk Business Centre, 130 Leith Walk, Edinburgh, EH6 5DT.

Historic Scotland
August 1997

the Scottish burgh survey

how to use this survey

summary

1 **Use the colour-coded map on the foldout at the back of the book figure 26** and/or the **general index** to locate a particular site (normally the site of a development proposal).

2 If the site is in a **blue area**, any development proposal is unlikely to affect significant archaeological remains. No action is needed.

3 **Green areas (light and dark green)** are designated as potentially archaeologically sensitive. If the site is in a green area, it is possible that a proposal involving ground disturbance may encounter archaeological remains. Seek appropriate archaeological advice as early as possible.

4 **Red areas** are Scheduled Ancient Monuments or properties in the care of the Secretary of State for Scotland, and are protected by law. Consult Historic Scotland.

5 Use the map on p 36 **figure 16** to determine into which area of the burgh the site falls (one of Areas 1–2), and turn to the relevant area in the **area by area assessment** for a fuller account (pp 37–57).

6 Use the **general index** and, if appropriate, the listing of **street names** (pp 69–71) for rapid access to information specific to a site, street or named feature of the town.

step 1

As a working manual, the first point of reference is the colour-coded map on the foldout at the back of the book **figure 26**.

The **red areas** are **protected by law**. Under the provisions of the Ancient Monuments and Archaeological Areas Act 1979 all development proposals which affect them require the prior written consent of the Secretary of state (Scheduled Monument Consent) in addition to any planning permission required. These provisions are administered on behalf of the Secretary of State by Historic Scotland. **All applications for planning permission which affect either the site or setting of a Scheduled Ancient Monument (red area) must be referred to Historic Scotland,** acting for the Secretary of State in terms of Section 15(j)(v) of the Town and Country Planning (General Development Procedure) (Scotland) Order 1992 and Section 5(e) of its Amendment (No. 2) Order 1994. *All enquiries regarding prospective development proposals in or adjacent to red areas should be referred to Historic Scotland for advice as early as possible.*

The **green areas (light and dark green)** are **potentially archaeologically sensitive** and may retain significant sub-surface archaeological information. *Consultation should take place with the local authority archaeologist where any development proposal or enquiry involving ground disturbance is being considered*, including car parks, road schemes, environmental improvements, landscaping and drainage schemes, as well as the usual range of development and re-development proposals in built-up areas. There is no necessity for a consultation where ground disturbance is not in prospect, such as applications for change of use of a building. There may, however, be a requirement to obtain *planning permission* or, in the case of a listed building, *listed building consent* or, if demolition works are proposed within a conservation area, *conservation area consent.* In such instances, early consultation with the staff of the local authority planning department will always be helpful.

If in doubt whether consultation is necessary, please refer to the local authority archaeologist and the local authority planning department. It is important to note that sub-surface disturbance within historic standing buildings may also affect archaeological remains, and that some standing buildings may retain archaeological features within their structures. Please seek advice as required.

The **blue areas** denote those parts of the historic burgh which **may be archaeologically sterile** and where archaeological consultation is probably not necessary. In practice, *there is rarely a hard dividing line between the green and the blue areas.* If in any doubt, check the account of the relevant area in the **area by area assessment** (*see* step 2), and seek archaeological advice as appropriate.

step 2

In this new series of burgh surveys, each survey has been organised locationally, in order to assist speedy consultation on any proposed development site. In the case of Coupar Angus, the historic core of the town has been divided into two arbitrary areas, Areas 1–2, which are shown on the plan on p 36 **figure 16**. The second step for the user, then, is to consult this plan and to determine into which area a specific enquiry falls.

step 3

Each area is assessed individually in the **area by area assessment** (pp 37–57). The commentary for each area is prefaced with a detailed plan of that area. Archaeological, historical, geographical and geological factors of particular relevance to the area are all discussed, and an assessment of the archaeological potential is made. For ease of reference, even if a dividing line between areas is shown as the middle of a street, discussion of the area includes any elements within the street up to the opposite frontage. The importance of an integrated approach to the historical and archaeological information is implicit in the design of this report: the history and archaeology are presented together on each page rather than consecutively.

This integrated, area-based approach has involved some repetition of information in the area by area assessment, in order that users are not required to cross-reference more than necessary when dealing with a specific enquiry. Although such repetition would not be normal in a work of interest to the general public, it was felt that it would be permissible here in order to facilitate the work of primary users: local authority planners and other curators of the archaeological resource.

historic standing buildings

historic buildings (pp 59–63) reinforces the above sections by providing basic historical and architectural information about the historic standing buildings of the town; where relevant, it also provides the area location and an assessment of the archaeological potential of specific buildings. *It should always be borne in mind that historic standing buildings may also contain archaeological remains, both beneath their floors and within their structures.* Some of these buildings may be listed and consequently subject to listed building control. Where listed buildings contain, or may contain, architecturally or archaeologically significant building fabric, the planning authority is obliged to make efforts to ensure that this is preserved and not adversely affected by proposed building works.

objectives for future fieldwork and research

Any report of this nature cannot be definitive. During its preparation, a series of archaeological and historical objectives for future fieldwork and research have been identified; these are listed at pp 65–7. They will be of particular interest to urban historians and archaeologists, and to those responsible for management of the archaeological resource in historic Coupar Angus.

referencing

The report contains a comprehensive **general index** as well as a listing of **street names** giving basic historical information and, where relevant, area location. A **bibliography** and a **glossary** of technical terms have also been included. Previous archaeological work and chance finds are listed and referenced at the end of both area assessments.
The data accumulated during preparation of this survey and draft copies of the completed work, as well as all unpublished reports of any small-scale excavations and watching briefs, are housed in the **National Monuments Record**, John Sinclair House, 16 Bernard Terrace, Edinburgh EH8 9NX, telephone *0131* 662 1456, facsimile *0131* 662 1477/1499.

full reference to this report

Dennison, E Patricia and Coleman, R 1997 *Historic Coupar Angus: the archaeological implications of development*, published by Historic Scotland in association with Scottish Cultural Press, Edinburgh. (Scottish Burgh Survey 1997).

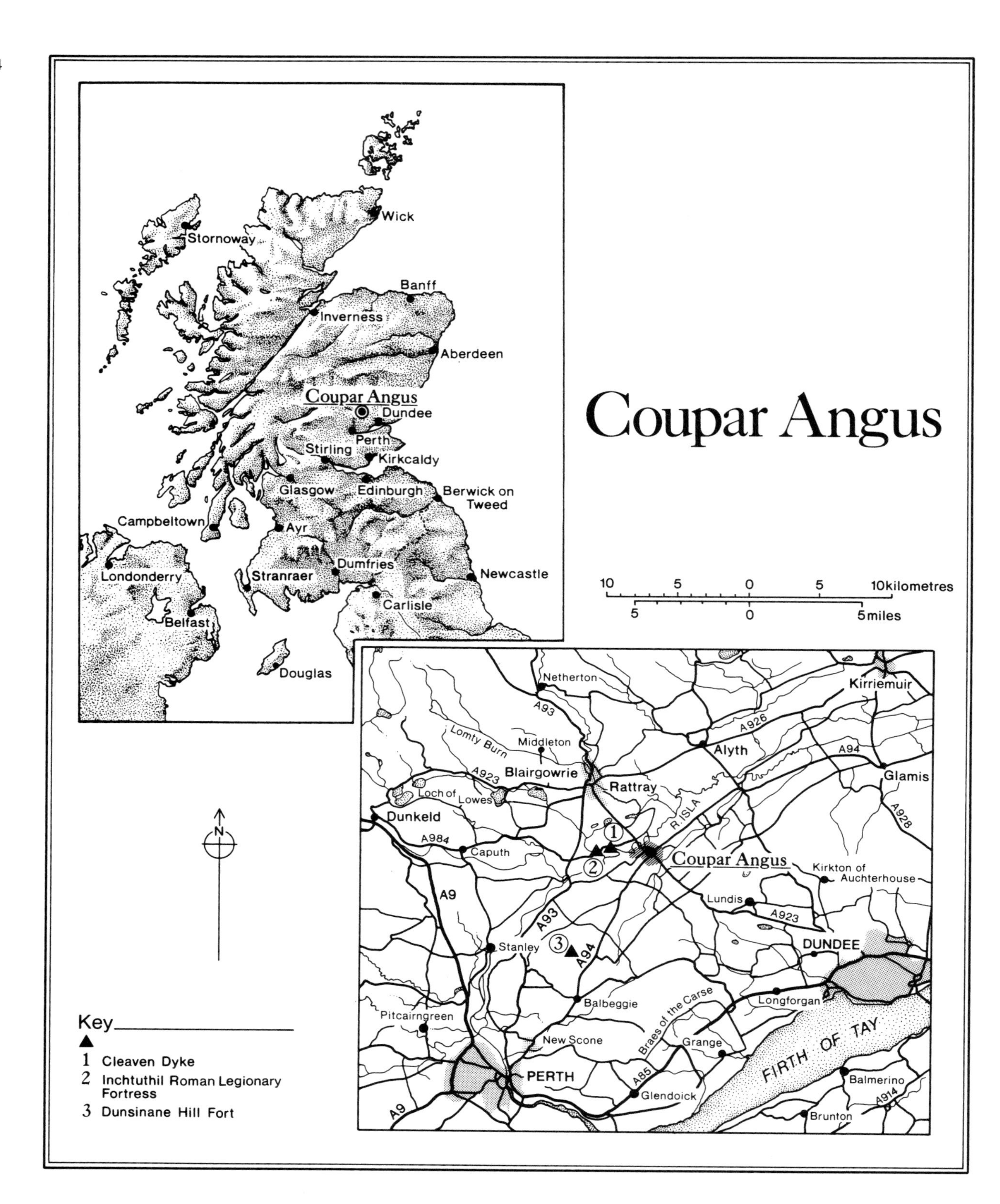

figure 1
Location of
Coupar Angus
© Crown Copyright

Coupar Angus: its site and setting

geography

Coupar Angus lies 20 km north-east of Perth and the same distance north-west of Dundee, in the agriculturally rich heartland of Strathmore **figure 1**. The burgh is situated on the southern side of the River Isla, adjacent to a pronounced U-shaped bend in the course of the river **figure 2**. The Grampian Mountains lie to the north and west of Strathmore, while to the south and east lie the Sidlaw Hills.

Strathmore is some 53 km long and at least 6.5 km wide and forms the main line of land communication through this part of Scotland, running north-east to south-west, parallel to the Grampian Mountains and the Sidlaw Hills. West of the Tay, this great valley is known as Strathearn.[1] The Sidlaw Hills also separate Strathmore from the Angus coastal plain to the east and the Carse of Gowrie to the south. Some of the richest agricultural land in the country is in Strathmore, but prior to the Improvements of the eighteenth and nineteenth centuries, it was an area of bog and shallow lochs with settlement mainly confined to gently sloping ground with good natural drainage, as at Coupar Angus.[2]

Despite its name, Coupar Angus used to be in Perth and Kinross District. Since 1 April 1996, it has been subsumed within the new Perth and Kinross unitary authority.

geology

South-east Scotland, in common with the rest of northern Britain, is enriched by complex geological actions including a wide variety of rocks and physical features. Tectonic movements along two major dislocations of the earth's crust, the Southern Uplands Fault and the Highland Boundary Fault, created three principal structural and physiographic divisions—the Highlands, the Midland Valley and the Southern Uplands.[3] Coupar Angus lies in the central division, the Midland Valley.

The Midland Valley nestles between the Highland Boundary Fault to the north, from Stonehaven to the Firth of Clyde at Helensburgh, and the Southern Upland Fault to the south, from Dunbar through New Cumnock to Glen App. Here, Old Red Sandstone and Carboniferous rocks are preserved within a trough 80 kilometres wide, resulting in a broad lowland tract of better farming and industrial development. Old Red Sandstone in the north passes eastwards beneath the rich soils of Strathmore and is separated by the hard igneous and volcanic rocks of the Sidlaw and Ochil Hills and Campsie Fells from the industrial south. Fairly intensive farming surrounds and serves the four-fifths of the population of Scotland which has concentrated around the coal-bearing rocks and oil-shales and their attendant heavy industry. Within this undulating lowland landscape, there are sharp irregularities of igneous rock forming conspicuous landmarks, for example: North Berwick Law and Traprain Law, near Haddington, in East Lothian; the dolerite hills of Fife; the Castle Rock of Stirling; the volcanics of the Bathgate Hills; and Arthur's Seat, in Edinburgh.[4]

The basic rock formations creating the landscape around Strathmore are Dalradian metamorphic rocks in the Grampian Mountains, Devonian Old Red Sandstones in Strathmore, and igneous rocks in the Sidlaw Hills.[5]

The broad, open valley of Strathmore extends from the River Tay to the Mearns (north of Montrose) and is underlain by soft sandstones worn down by fluvio-glacial activity. The area around Coupar Angus is drained south-westwards by the River Isla and, to the north, by its main tributary, the River Ericht.[7] The River Isla meanders through Strathmore before meeting the Tay near Meikleour, whilst the River Ericht cuts a deep gorge through the Highland Boundary Fault north of Blairgowrie before joining the Isla at Coupar Grange.[8]

The main features of the present-day landscape were probably in place by the end of the Tertiary period (around 2 million years ago), but were considerably re-shaped during the subsequent Quaternary period (which includes the Ice Age and extends up to the present day). Boulder clay, sands and gravels were deposited by the meltwaters during the retreat of the ice, and on the lower ground these deposits gave rise to drumlins and glacial drainage-channels.

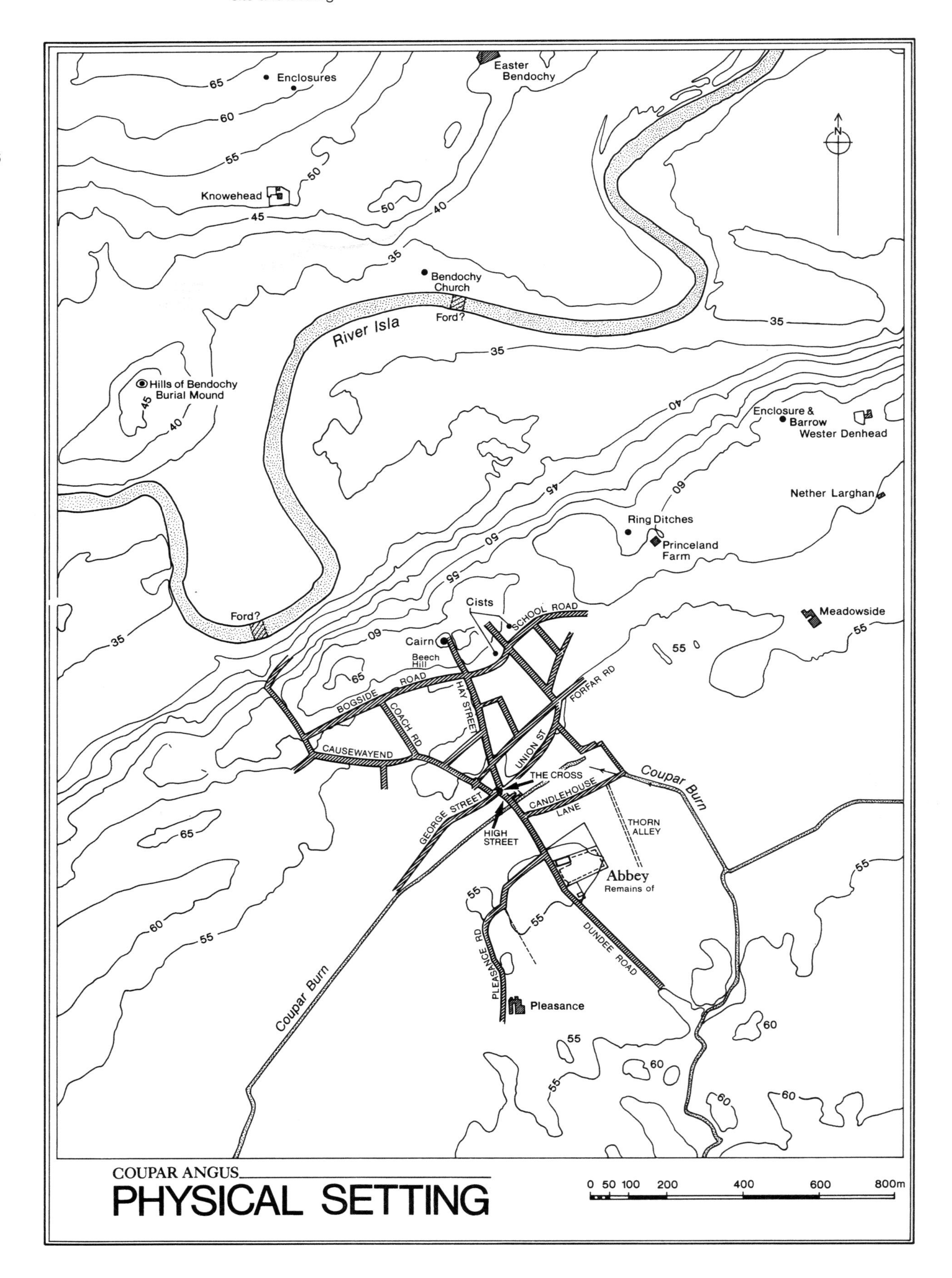

figure 2
The physical setting
of Coupar Angus

figure 3
Coupar Angus
from the air
1983
© Crown Copyright

soils, climate and land use

The varying landscape is reflected in the types of agriculture practised: hill farming in the glens of the Grampian Mountains and on the higher tracts of the Sidlaws; stock farming with a little arable land along the Highland boundary fault and on the other ranges of hills; and arable farming and feeding farms in Strathmore, Strathearn and the Angus coastal plain.[9]

Much of the valley of Strathmore is undulating lowland, lying between 40 m and 100 m OD, but with some low, rounded hills to the south-west. Fluvio-glacial deposits comprising sands, gravels and clays mask the underlying rocks and give rise to a range of soil types.[10] The sand and gravel sub-soils produce naturally free-draining land, whilst the clay sub-soil tends to retain water. The latter soils, which are concentrated in the south-east of Strathmore and along the lower slopes of the Sidlaw Hills, have been extensively improved since the early nineteenth century.[11]

physical setting and the topography of the burgh

Coupar Angus lies in an area of low lying ground, south of a pronounced U-shaped bend in the course of the River Isla **figures 2 & 3**. The modern town is divided in two by the

figure 4
Aerial view of the abbey precinct 1983

Coupar Burn. The newly opened A94 relief road, which runs along the south side of the burn, reinstates the line of the former railway over which it was built.

The precinct of a Cistercian abbey was located south of the Coupar Burn **figures 4, 16 & 17**, with the main complex of church and cloisters situated on slightly raised ground. Little remains of the abbey; much of the area once within its precinct has gradually been infilled by housing, a process which began after the Reformation.

Medieval settlement contemporary with the abbey was north of the Coupar Burn, at the foot of a gentle slope. The modern street layout of this part of town has its origins in the medieval period. Its convergent street plan, where a number of streets meet at The Cross, probably respects the site of the main north gateway into the monastic precinct, and of an early market place which developed here. Causewayend, a narrow, twisting street, is said to have been the main route to and from the crossing over the Isla near Butterybank, but a more likely fording point is east of Bendochy Church (*see* p 24) **figure 19**.

At the northern end of the town a long ridge, on which the suburb of Beech Hill is situated, separates the town from the River Isla. From here, the ground falls gently towards the Coupar Burn to the south and the Isla to the north.

The most significant addition to the town plan at Coupar Angus is the new A94 relief road. Although it largely reinstates the old railway line, it has effectively blocked off access from The Cross and High Street into the former abbey precinct. Two new roundabouts at the east end of the town, built over the disused railway's goods yard, take traffic on to Forfar and Blairgowrie.

notes

1 B Walker & G Ritchie, *Exploring Scotland's Heritage: Fife and Tayside* (Edinburgh, 1993), 9.
2 *Ibid*, 11.
3 C J Brown & B M Shipley, *Soil Survey of Scotland: South East Scotland. Soil and Land Capability for Agriculture* (The Macaulay Institute for Soil Research, Aberdeen, 1982), 2. The three major land divisions (Highlands, Midland Valley and Southern Uplands) follow J B Sissons, *The Geomorphology of the British Isles: Scotland* (London, 1976).
4 E Edmonds, *The Geological Map, an Anatomy of a Landscape* (HMSO, London, 1983), 18.
5 Walker & Ritchie, *Fife and Tayside*, 9.
6 Royal Commission on the Ancient and Historical Monuments of Scotland, *South-East Perth: an Archaeological Landscape* (Edinburgh, 1994), 2.
7 *Ibid*, 2.
8 *Ibid*, 2.
9 Walker & Ritchie, *Fife and Tayside*, 10–11.
10 RCAHMS, *South-East Perth*, 2.
11 *Ibid*, 2.

archaeological and historical background

pp 11–35

archaeological and historical background

A limited amount of archaeological work has been undertaken within the historic core of Coupar Angus, particularly in the last few years, and a number of stray finds have also been reported. Further afield, a wide range of prehistoric and historic sites and finds have been recorded from around the burgh. A basic introduction to the prehistory and early history of the area is included in this book in order to place the sites and finds in context and to provide a broader framework within which to study the origins of the burgh of Coupar Angus.

The Royal Commission on the Ancient and Historical Monuments of Scotland recently published the results of its comprehensive survey of south-east Perthshire in *South-East Perth: an Archaeological Landscape*. Published in 1994, it provides a companion volume to the Royal Commission's *North-East Perth* (1990). Both volumes incorporate the results of fieldwork and aerial photography, together with maps and drawings, and detail the rich archaeological and historical heritage of this part of Scotland, Strathmore in particular.

prehistory

The earliest settlement of Scotland occurred around 7,000 BC, when much of Scotland was covered in dense woodland which supported a rich variety of game, particularly red deer. The few Mesolithic (literally meaning Middle Stone Age) settlements known in Scotland tend to be found along the coast line and river banks. These communities were 'hunter-gatherers', who ate fish and shellfish, followed herds of woodland game through the seasons, and supplemented their diet with wild plants and berries. Their semi-nomadic existence has left few archaeological traces, although shell middens and flint tools are common finds along former river and coast lines. There is no evidence for Mesolithic activities in the immediate vicinity of Coupar Angus.

Around 3,500 BC, people began to live a more settled existence in response to changes in the environment, including more favourable soil conditions, and to ideas introduced from continental Europe. Large areas of woodland were cleared by burning and trees were cut down with stone tools, livestock was kept and the land was farmed for crops. Again, few traces of these Neolithic (literally meaning New Stone Age) settlements survive, but the landscape still bears evidence of the presence of these people, in the form of their ritual enclosures (including henges) and burial mounds.

Ritual is strongly evidenced in the lives of these early farming groups, particularly in their treatment of the dead, who were buried in monumental tombs. These communal stone-built chambered cairns or barrows constructed of wood and turf sometimes contained large numbers of burials. There is considerable regional variation in the types and styles of these monuments, no doubt reflecting local traditions and perhaps the origins of the societies which used them.[1] The tombs probably became a focus for ritual where elaborate ceremonies took place, perhaps in celebration of the ancestors. No chambered cairns are known from this part of Strathmore, but a variety of other types of ceremonial and ritual monuments have been identified. One of the most enigmatic is the Cleaven Dyke, near Blairgowrie **figure 1**. Long thought to have been associated with the Roman legionary fortress at nearby Inchtuthil, recent excavation and survey in fact revealed it to be Neolithic.[2] Its most obvious feature is a pair of parallel ditches on either side of a long and complex mound. This ceremonial avenue probably links with other ritual sites; a growing number of cropmark features have been identified by aerial photography in the vicinity, suggesting that the Cleaven Dyke was at the centre, if not the actual focus, of an important area of Neolithic ceremonial activity **figure 1**. It is an extremely rare above-ground survival of a linear monument from this period and it is quite remarkable that it is near complete.

By about 2,500 BC changes in society were gradually taking place and monuments such as stone circles were erected, apparently incorporating an awareness of the rising and setting of the sun and moon in their design.[3] The tradition of monumental tombs

figure 5
Aerial view of Beech Hill House excavations 1989
© Crown Copyright: RCAHMS

containing large numbers of burials waned in favour of a new trend for single grave burials. Bronze Age people also developed new styles of pottery, unenclosed settlements and metal-working.

A number of Bronze Age burials have been found in this part of Strathmore, representing two different traditions of burial: inhumation and cremation. Both traditions usually contain the body, or an urn containing cremated remains, within a small stone-lined cist set beneath a stone cairn, although some cremation urns were placed in a pit. Some were single, isolated burials but others were part of larger cemeteries. Cairns were often reused and can contain a number of later burials inserted into the flanks or top of the mound.

Several cist burials have been found in Coupar Angus, and one of the few modern excavations of a Bronze Age burial mound took place at Beech Hill House **figure 5** in 1989 (*see* pp 53–4).[4] What looked to be a rather unassuming mound contained a complex sequence of structures and burials of different dates and a wealth of grave goods, including food vessels, a bronze pin, two bone artefacts, a pommel and a toggle **figure 6**. The site was the focus of burial activity over a long period, from at least the beginning of the second millennium BC, and its complexity is a valuable reminder of the inherent difficulties facing archaeologists trying to date and characterise sites from survey alone. Another burial mound, protected as a Scheduled Ancient Monument, can be seen north of the River Isla at Hills of Bendochy **figure 2**.

Despite the abundance of evidence for funerary monuments and rich burials in the Neolithic and Bronze Ages, knowledge of the subsistence base which supported these

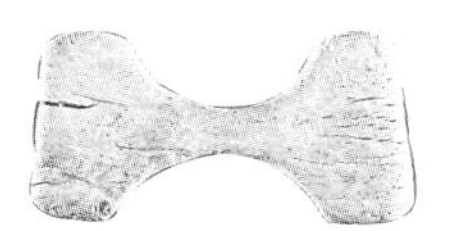

figure 6
Bronze Age bone toggle *above, actual size* and food vessels *right, half size* from Beech Hill House

societies and the settlements in which they lived is rather poor.[5] By the late Bronze Age and early Iron Age, however, settlements begin to dominate the archaeological landscape. These include numerous fortified settlements, ranging from large hillforts to enclosed villages and isolated single-family dwellings. The end of the Bronze Age, around 600 BC, was a time of considerable change. Iron tools begin to appear in the archaeological record. Society seems generally to have been more competitive, with the emergence of tribal groups perhaps competing for territory and natural resources. Less defensive types of settlement also existed, however, and indeed the vast majority of sites of this period in Strathmore are undefended, open villages. Local society may have been becoming more highly organised and controlled, thus enabling undefended Iron Age farming landscapes to emerge in the later 1st millennium BC.

The survey technique of aerial photography has led to the identification of a huge number of previously unknown archaeological sites. These discoveries are gradually filling in some of the gaps in our knowledge of prehistoric settlement. In Strathmore alone, large numbers of enclosed and unenclosed settlements have been identified, which have greatly increased our awareness of the complexity of settlement patterns and the density of Iron Age settlement in lowland arable landscapes. Many of these are Scheduled Ancient Monuments.

later prehistory and the Roman period

Recent archaeological fieldwork indicates that Strathmore supported a sizeable Iron Age population,[6] but our knowledge of contemporary native activities during the Roman occupation of Strathmore is limited. One relatively well-studied settlement feature common in this part of Scotland, however, is the souterrain. A souterrain is a curving, stone-built underground passage or gallery, roofed with either stone slabs or timbers, and possibly used for storing food or sheltering animals. They are sometimes called 'Picts' houses', but they are in fact much earlier and date from the late first millennium BC to the early first millennium AD. Excavations of souterrains, notably Newmill in Perthshire, revealed structural remains of unusually large houses adjacent to the passage, through which access to the souterrain was obtained. Several of these sites are known in the Coupar Angus area, including at least two at Mudhall, near Coupar Grange. Probably the best example in Scotland is at Pitcur, some 4 km south of Coupar Angus.

Other types of native settlement were more defensive and one of the most spectacular in the area, commanding a wide sweep of country across the southern end of Strathmore, is the fort at Dunsinane Hill **figure 1**, approximately 5 km north-east of Balbeggie.[7] Although spoiled in appearance by excavations in 1799 and again in 1854, the fort is still an imposing citadel, enclosed by a wall up to 9 m thick and surrounded by two outer stone ramparts. The citadel almost certainly replaced an earlier fort on the summit, indicating that settlement on this hill probably spanned the later prehistoric to the early historic periods, apparently with a break during the Roman occupation.

It was this Iron Age society which the Romans encountered in the first century AD. According to Ptolemy, the classical geographer whose map of the Roman world was compiled around AD 140, it is possible that Strathmore fell within the territorial domain of either the Venicones or the Caledonii.[8]

The Roman conquest of Britain commenced with the invasion of the Emperor Claudius in AD 43. However, it took another two generations before Roman armies reached the area now known as Scotland. The main invasion occurred under the governor Gnaeus Julius Agricola. Much of our knowledge of the early history of Roman Britain results from his biography, written by his son-in-law, the distinguished historian Cornelius Tacitus. Chosen as the new governor probably in AD 77, Agricola first campaigned in Wales before moving into north Britain in AD 78. With an army which may have numbered as many as 20,000 men (based on the four legions available in Britain, plus auxiliary troops),[9] he advanced through southern Scotland as far as the Tay. There is no record of any opposition on the part of the native tribes, but Tacitus did note that bad weather hindered progress during that season's campaigning. The following year was spent consolidating and garrisoning the new frontier zone; this included the establishment of forts in the newly conquered territory. In particular, Agricola established a line of forts in the valley between the Forth and the Clyde.[10] In AD 81, Agricola mounted a campaign into south-west Scotland, while in AD 82 he advanced beyond the Forth into Strathmore. This, his sixth campaign, culminated in the defeat of the Caledonians under Calgacus in the battle of Mons Graupius in AD 83. The site of this famous battle has been the source of much debate but probably lies somewhere in north-east Scotland.[11] This was the climax of Agricola's governorship and, shortly afterwards, he returned to Rome.

It was left to Agricola's successor (whose name is unknown) to consolidate his advances, with a system of roads and forts established beyond the Forth and deep into Strathmore. This included forts strategically placed at the mouths of the Highland glens, such as Fendoch, Dalginross and Bochastle, but the nerve-centre was the 53 acre (21.5 ha) legionary fortress at Inchtuthil on the Tay **figure 1**. The date of its construction is uncertain, but it seems likely that it was not begun until after the governorship of Agricola. Whether further military campaigns were undertaken or intended is uncertain, and Inchtuthil was deliberately demolished by the army before its construction was even completed.[12] The reason for this change in policy was a series of military disasters in continental Europe, and troops had to be redeployed there from elsewhere in the Empire. As a result, all the forts north of the line from Newstead to Glenlochar were abandoned about AD 87. By the turn of the century, the Romans had fallen back as far as the Tyne–Solway line, where a frontier was established, with its principal forts at Carlisle and Corbridge, connected by a main road now known as the Stanegate.

In the early AD 120s, it was a line slightly further north of this frontier that was chosen by the Emperor Hadrian for the construction of a massive barrier of stone and turf, now known as Hadrian's Wall. As the northern frontier of the empire it was short-lived, for in AD 138 Hadrian's successor, Antoninus Pius, ordered his army to advance into central Scotland and begin construction of a second great barrier, the Antonine Wall. Construction of the Wall appears to have commenced after a victory in AD 142 (recorded in a coin issue late in that year), and building probably continued into the AD 150s. It is possible that Antoninus' motives for building the wall were similar to those behind Claudius' invasion of Britain in AD 43—the need for a military victory to bolster the reputation of a new emperor.

The Wall stretched for some 60 km between Bo'ness on the Forth and Old Kilpatrick on the Clyde, with forts roughly every two miles and fortlets at every mile. New forts were also established south of the Wall, many on or close by sites of abandoned forts. Some forts were also established north of the Wall, up to the Tay, and some earlier forts were reoccupied, including Bertha on the Tay near Perth. Trouble on the northern frontier in the mid to late 150s may have led to the abandonment of some forts, and perhaps the whole system, but many were refurbished or rebuilt within a relatively short time.[13] This re-occupation proved to be temporary, as most of the forts in Scotland were again abandoned sometime in the decade AD 160 to 170, and the army withdrew to the line of Hadrian's Wall, which was now once again the northern frontier of Roman Britain. Some forts in Dumfriesshire and up to the Tweed were retained as outposts, but by about AD 180 even these were abandoned, with the exception of Netherby, Bewcastle, High Rochester and Risingham.

There was one final episode in the history of Roman Scotland. For a variety of reasons the Emperor Septimius Severus, together with his sons Caracalla and Geta, arrived in Britain to mount a major campaign in the north, specifically against two tribes—the Maeatae, whose territory seems to have been Stirlingshire, Strathearn and Strathmore, and the Caledonians who were based further north.[14] Probably accompanied by a fleet, Severus and his army advanced beyond Hadrian's Wall in AD 208, through eastern Scotland and up the east coast. Despite taking the title *Britannicus*, 'conqueror of Britain', Severus' celebrations were short-lived, for a major rebellion occurred in the following year. Construction work on a new fortress at Carpow, on the Tay near Newburgh, suggests that the Romans intended to stay. Severus died in AD 211. His son Caracalla succeeded him and immediately returned to Rome, abandoning the Scottish conquests.[15] Hadrian's Wall was again reinstated as the northern frontier of the province, with some forts garrisoned in the Cheviots as out-posts. By the late third century AD the Picts—probably a new power grouping amongst the tribes—and others were putting increasing pressure on the northern frontier. Hadrian's Wall appears to have been garrisoned until the early years of the fifth century AD, before Britain was finally abandoned by Rome.

Roman Strathmore

No certain traces of Agricola's campaigns have come to light as yet, and the known sites of that period probably all date to the process of occupation following the victory at Mons Graupius.[16] There were two lines of forts north of the Forth occupied in the first century AD. One lay along the edge of the Highlands, with a fort tactically placed at the mouth of each glen. The other line lay along the road running north-eastwards from Doune at the crossing of the Teith.

The legionary fortress at Inchtuthil lay at the mouth of one of the most important access points to the Highlands, the Dunkeld gorge, the route taken today by the A9 road **figure 1**. The fort and fortlet at Cargill lay close to Inchtuthil but probably on the route taken by the Roman road. The relationship between Cargill and Inchtuthil is not known; they may have been occupied at the same time as they served different functions. The fort at Cargill guarded a crossing on the Isla and was probably occupied prior to, or during, the construction of the Inchtuthil legionary fortress. Once Inchtuthil was built, the fort may have been abandoned in favour of a smaller garrison at the fortlet, situated some 250 m away.[17] The existence of a signal-station or watch-tower at Black Hill further complicates the situation.

All these military installations were abandoned *c* AD 87, apparently peacefully. The defences and internal structures of Inchtuthil, for example, were systematically dismantled and any materials likely to be of use to the native tribes buried.

During the Antonine period, Strathmore lay beyond the most northerly outpost fort; however, the Romans did have treaty relations with the Caledonii and Maeatae in AD 197, so the area was still very much in the Roman sphere of activity. It was not until the early third century AD that Roman troops are known to have operated again in this area, with the Severan campaigns of AD 208–211 against the northern tribes. The course of these campaigns can be traced from the distribution of a series of large temporary camps, built to accommodate the army on the move. They are often identified only by aerial photography, and a number have been found in Strathmore. Lintrose, south of Coupar

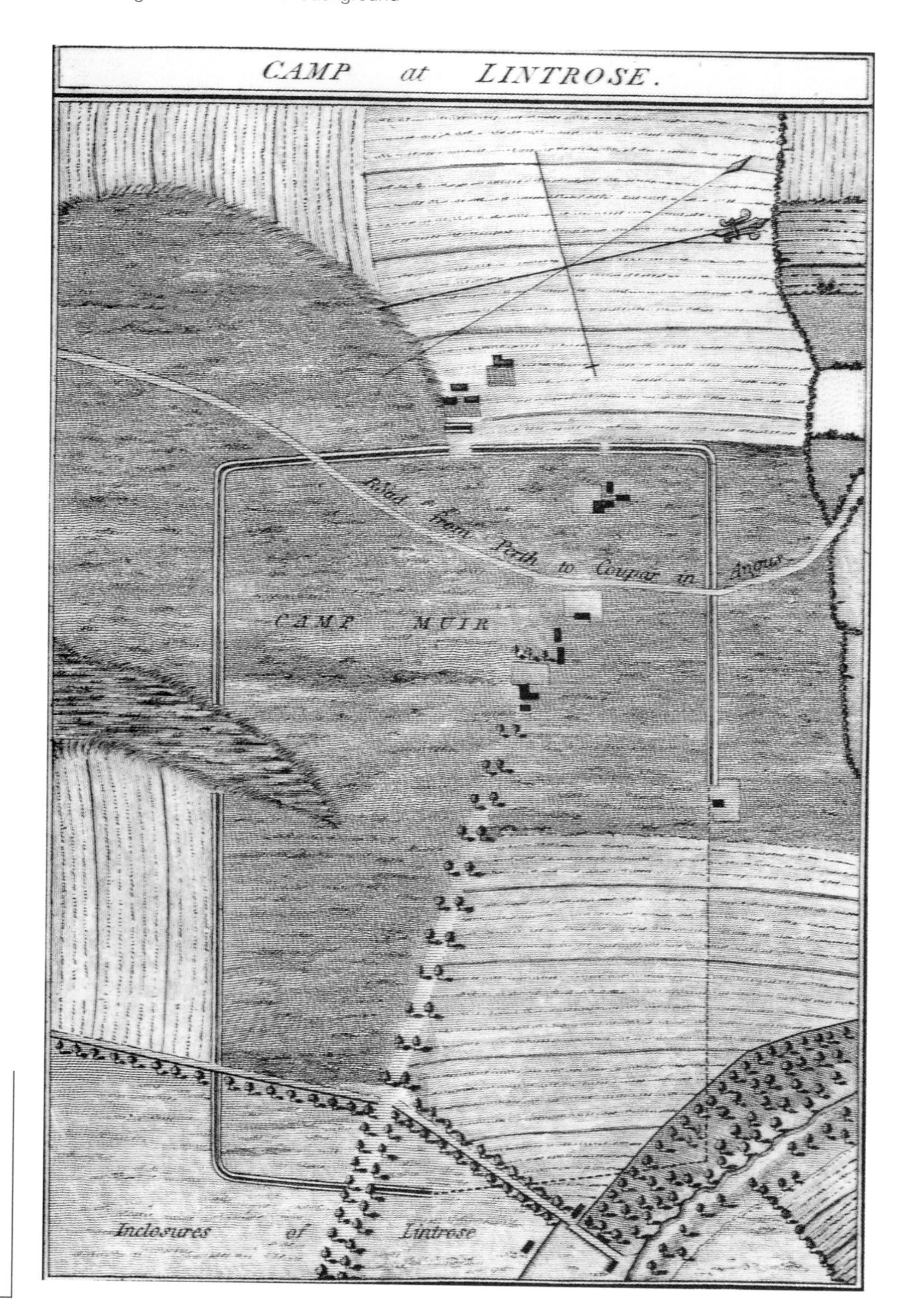

figure 7
Roman temporary camp at Lintrose, from W Roy *Military Antiquities*, 1793, plate xiv © Crown Copyright: RCAHMS

Angus, was first identified and recorded in the eighteenth century **figure 7**, but only short stretches of the defences still survive. There is also a tradition of a camp in Coupar Angus itself, within which the medieval abbey precinct was later laid out **figure 4**. The dimensions of the earthwork (*see* pp 38–9 *and* 44–5), again first recorded in the eighteenth century, would, however, fit the proportions of a Flavian period camp rather than a Severan one,[18] if indeed it was Roman in date. At other times treaties probably governed the relationship between the peoples of this area and the Roman empire.

the early historic period

There were major changes in the political and religious organisation of Scotland in the period after the withdrawal of the Romans, and four distinct territorial groupings or

figure 8
Pictish cross slab, Kettins Churchyard 1988
© Crown Copyright: RCAHMS

kingdoms appear in the historical and archaeological record. The mainland and islands north of the Forth and Clyde estuaries were inhabited by the Picts, descendants of the indigenous Iron Age tribes. A number of smaller tribes had been absorbed into two confederations, the Caledonii and the Maeatae, and by the end of the third century AD these peoples were first referred to collectively as the Picts. Strathclyde was home to the Britons, whose capital lay on the north side of the Clyde at Alcluith (Dumbarton Rock), and on their north-western border were the *Scoti*. Originally from north-east Ireland, by the fifth century AD they had established the kingdom of Dalriada in Argyll. Finally, the Anglian kings of Northumbria were in control of much of south-east Scotland.

It was the *Scoti* who eventually dominated, but not until the mid ninth century AD, when Kenneth mac Alpin and his descendants established royal, political and cultural supremacy over the Pictish kingdom. The *Scoti*, in fact, had been gradually drifting eastwards to settle in Pictland, partly in response to increased Viking attacks in northern Dalriada and along the Atlantic seaboard. The Picts had also suffered at the hands of the Norsemen, losing control of both Orkney and Shetland. By the early eleventh century AD, the Scottish kings had also gained control of Strathclyde and Northumbrian Lothian.

Few Pictish settlement sites have been identified; the so-called Pitcarmick houses and enigmatic cropmarks provide tantalising glimpses of this period, referred to by some as the Dark Ages. The Picts of Strathmore, however, left a startling heritage of carved stones,[19] designs in the form of birds, animals and fish or more abstract symbols and figures, incised on great, monolithic stones. The meaning of the scenes and symbols depicted on these stones is open to interpretation, as is their function. They might have been boundary markers, memorial stones or tombstones, for example.[20] Often referred to as Class I stones, they probably date from the sixth and seventh centuries AD.

From his base at Whithorn, St Ninian is reputed to have led the first Christian mission to southern Pictland in the early fifth century AD, but monks from the monastery of Iona (established by St Columba in 563) may have been the first to make an impact in this area. The increasing influence of Christianity inspired another, slightly later class of sculpture, known as Class II stones. These free-standing cross-slabs appeared, in greater numbers, from the late seventh or eighth century AD. Carved in relief on carefully shaped stones, characteristically these bear a cross and other Christian iconography on one side, and symbols on the other, with frequent depictions of Pictish aristocrats involved in the noble pursuit of hunting. These testify to the important role of the Church in contemporary society, particularly after the activities of the reforming king Nechtán, in the early eighth century. Strathmore is exceptionally rich in Pictish stones and important collections can be seen at Aberlemno, Fowlis Wester, Glamis and Meigle, for example. In the Coupar Angus area, an example of a cross-slab can be seen in Kettins churchyard **figure 8**.

1100–1607

Although there is no firm documentary evidence of settlement in the Coupar Angus area in the early twelfth century, there was a royal manor at Coupar Angus by at least the reign of David I (1124–53).[21] This would suggest some sort of settlement in the locality, and the area was already known by the name of Coupar. There have been various suggestions as to the derivation of the name 'Coupar': they include the Gaelic 'Cul-bhar', meaning the end, or back, of a bank or height;[22] or 'Cobhair', a sanctuary or place of monkish refuge; or the Flemish 'Copar', meaning one who exchanges commodities;[23] or the vernacular 'coo byre'; or after St Cuthbert.[24] It represents, however, an early P-celtic compound with the same meaning as 'aber', that is 'a confluence'. It occurs in Dalfouber, near Edzell; Cupar and Drumcooper in Fife; as well as in Coupar Angus and Couttie (Cuppermacul-tin) in Bendochy.[25] In 1159, when Malcolm IV (1156–65) allocated territory for the foundation of a Cistercian monastery at Coupar Angus, on the advice of his uncle, Waltheof, abbot of Melrose,[26] he set aside 'the royal manor of Coupar in Gowrie'.[27] The existence of a royal grange in this vicinity would, at the very least, suggest the presence of a group of agricultural workers and, perhaps, even an agrarian community. Had the *manerium* been waste or deserted, it would be expected that the documentation would have said so.

There may also have been a parish church in the locality. When the Cistercians arrived at Coupar Angus, the bishop of St Andrews surrendered all his rights to this church in favour of the new abbey. The 'foundation charter' of the abbey, dating to 1161 or 1162, suggests that the church was the kirk of Coupar Angus;[28] but whether it was in Coupar Angus itself or possibly in Bendochy is unclear.[29] A parish church, and one which the bishop of St Andrews considered worthy of a special gesture, would, however, imply the existence of some nearby parishioners.[30]

It has been claimed, on the other hand, that the Cistercian rule favoured *novalia*, or unbroken land, for spiritual isolation; this would suggest that the twelfth-century pre-Cistercian Coupar landscape was wild, uncultivated countryside.[31] But, in reality, it seems that the order preferred good agricultural land which might often support a pre-existing settlement. This was mostly the case in continental Europe;[32] and also in England, in the late twelfth century, it was maintained that the Cistercians 'raze villages and churches ... and level everything before the ploughshare'.[33] An assessment of the recorded Cistercian granges in England and Wales found that only 40 per cent were established on waste or marginal land.[34] Rather than establishing themselves on virgin land, the Cistercians usually moved into rich agricultural areas, which often maintained an existing farming community. This community was then assimilated into the order's network of granges.[35]

Although none of these factors prove definitively that there was a community at Coupar before the arrival of the Cistercians, it does seem quite probable that some form of settlement pre-dated the monastery. Once established, the Cistercian complex would have attracted further settlers, who came partly to benefit from the protective aura of the monastic complex but also to fulfil the demand for supplies and commodities created by a monastic establishment, even if it was largely self-sufficient. Although lay-brothers would have formed an essential part of the monastery, a workforce would also have been needed and would have been drawn from the local people. There is reference to one lay brother, clearly a local with the name of Gilesperda (possibly a misrendering of Gille-pedair or Gille-phadruig), in Jocelin's *Life of Waltheof* written in the late twelfth century.[36] The establishment of a Cistercian monastery in Coupar was to have a profound effect on the settlement pattern of the area.

The principal charter of Malcolm IV, granting his whole land of Coupar, with all its appurtenances, to the Cistercians may be dated to sometime in the period 1161 until 13 September 1162. It has been argued, however, that 1161 is the more probable dating and that Cistercians from Melrose were established at Coupar well before September 1162. Two years later, a full convent of at least twelve monks arrived and an abbot, Fulk, was appointed.[37]

Sometime between 1173 and 1178, William I (1165–1214) bestowed a further grant of land: half a ploughgate of land 'ad situm abbacie sue faciendum'.[38] This latter grant is interesting. The immediate suggestion is that the abbey was to be built on land not already in the possession of the Cistercians. This would mean that the royal manor of Coupar did not contain the intended site of the abbey. There are two potential implications. The grant may have been merely extending the area of land already given by Malcolm IV; or a gift of land in an area quite separate from the manor of Coupar Angus was now being made. If the latter is the case, it has to be presumed that the Cistercian monks from Melrose settled firstly on the royal manor and later moved to the area now known as Coupar. The manor and the abbey site may not have been far distant, but the possibility exists that they were distinct and separate places. The extensive complex by Coupar Grange, north of the Isla, recently highlighted by aerial photography, may be a candidate for this early site.

It seems that the monks were not long in establishing themselves. In 1186, rebels against the king, the McWilliams, led by Adam (Aed or Heth), son of Donald, son of Malcolm MacHeth, were pursued by the earl of Atholl into the abbey of Coupar Angus and killed there, in defiance of the laws of sanctuary.[39] The act was perpetrated before the altar, which might suggest that the church was already built, and fifty-eight others were burned in the abbot's quarters.[40] This does not necessarily mean that the monastic complex was fully constructed. Such an undertaking could have taken decades; but it may be significant that the confirmation of a charter of 1196x1207, perhaps 1199, made by Thomas, son of Malcolm of Lundie, specified that if he died in Scotland his body was to be buried at Coupar Angus in 'the cloister before the church door'.[41] This also implies that the cloister and church of the monastery were built by this date. It seems clear that construction work was on-going at the turn of the twelfth and thirteenth centuries: a charter of 1190x1214 confirmed grants of rights in the woods of one Peter Polloc, which suggests the supply of building materials. Malcolm, earl of Atholl, also granted timber from his forests, which were to be used in the construction of the abbey buildings.[42] Whether this was a reflection of a need to repair the damage done by the earl and his supporters in 1186 is unclear. The dedication of the church to St Mary in 1233[43] would suggest that by this date the main work on the church was complete, or nearing completion.

The completed abbey complex would have consisted of the normal conventual buildings: church, cloister, residence for the abbot, sleeping accommodation for the monks, refectory, guest house and sundry offices. It has been suggested that Cistercian houses also needed a range of further buildings, such as stables, brew- houses, bake-houses and metal-working premises.[44] Amongst Coupar's retainers were a baker, brewer and store-master, which gives some clues to the associated workshops;[45] although the store-master, as well as the fowler, land-stewards, foresters, bullock-herds and warreners, may have worked outwith the abbey precinct. Archaeological work has indicated that there may have been a wool-house at Fountains in North Yorkshire.[46] It is quite possible that Coupar also had one as early as the thirteenth century: Douai received wool, valued at £35, from the abbey of 'Cupre'.[47] There is little evidence, however, of the precise lay-out of the complex, but it is known that there were various gardens within its walls. One George Tailzeour was contracted in 1542 to tend the herb garden and the orchard, clean the fish tanks and provide kale and herbs for the abbot. There was also a mustard yard; possibly other gardens as further gardeners were also employed;[48] and a dovecot yard.[49] A charter of 1565 describes the complex as 'the place houssis yards orcheardis'.[50] There was also an outer yard to the abbey, set at the west side of the complex[51] and a porter's lodge.[52] In 1592/3, there was noted the 'tour, fortalice and maner place of the ... abbay witht the haill orcheardis, yeardis, myln, etc'.[53] Although not precise, all of these references suggest an extensive establishment and the present Precinct Street may well reflect only part of the site occupied by the monastery. The exact dimensions of the abbey complex, however, are unknown (pp 38–41).

The abbey received many gifts in the first century and a half of its existence. The crown was a generous benefactor and so were local landed families, in particular the Hays of Errol and the earls of Atholl.[54] Grants commonly included: lands and their associated privileges, such as fishings, collection of peat and grazings; patronage of churches and their revenues; money; rights of way; and candle wax for the monastery church.[55] The abbey was soon to possess endowments close by, as well as far afield, in Aberdeenshire (Murthly) and Banffshire (Alveth, now Alvah);[56] granges were established at Aberbothrie, Balbrogie, Carse Grange, Drimmie, Keithick, Tullyfergus, Kincreith, Airlie and Coupar Angus itself;[57] and the abbey also held properties in the burgh of Dundee,[58] some from as early as the late twelfth/early thirteenth century.[59] The list of jewels and plate taken from the abbey in 1296 by Edward I of England (1272–1307) confirms its exceptional wealth.[60] Such an important and wealthy abbey naturally hosted royalty: in 1246, Alexander II (1214–49) **figure 9**;[61] Robert I (1306–29) was at the abbey in November 1313[62] and spent Christmas there in 1316;[63] David II (1329–71) was a guest in June 1341;[64] and in the winter of 1378 Robert II (1371–90) made two visits.[65]

The abbey also had an impact on more ordinary people. As a wealthy landowner which exported its produce overseas and also had an agricultural surplus, its function as the focus of a market had implications for the surrounding hinterland. From its

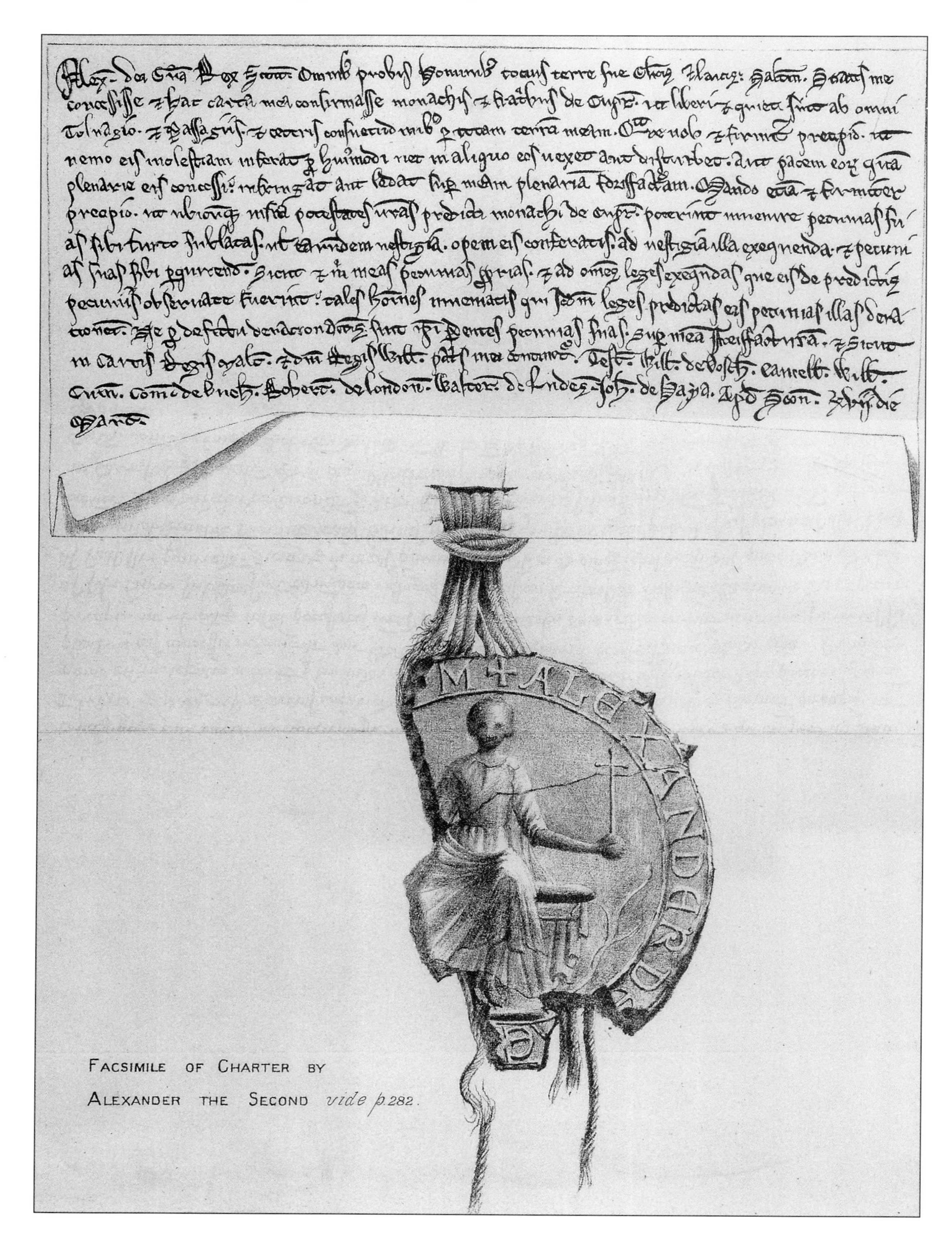

figure 9
Charter of Alexander II, King of Scots (1214–49) to Coupar Angus monastery.

foundation, the abbey had the liberty to buy and sell for its own needs throughout the kingdom free of payment of toll.[66] How soon a market was established at its gate is unclear, but by 1352 the fair at Coupar Abbey was proving detrimental to Dundee's trade[67] In 1359, David II issued a charter to Dundee prohibiting Coupar Angus, Kettins, Kirriemuir and Alyth to hold markets since they were within the liberty of Dundee,[68] which had the sole right to sell wool and skins and deal with foreign merchants within the sheriffdom of Forfar.[69] It seems that these measures were largely ignored and the market continued; the bishop of Dunkeld, for example, bought boards for a church roof there in 1506.[70] Fruit trees were also purchased for the king's residence at Stirling, but whether at the market or not is unclear.[71]

Coupar's market was held 'at the gate of the monastery every Friday'.[72] The red cross, which was probably the market cross, stood to the north of the abbey precincts[73] and functioned as the focal point of settlement.[74] An important landmark, it was used as the dividing line of the barony of Keithick, thus placing Coupar Angus, or Baitscheill (Beech Hill), at the centre of the barony.[75] Baitscheill appears frequently in the abbey's records from the fifteenth century; it may have designated the whole area to the north of the abbey as far as the Isla.[76]

A regular market would have attracted not only traders, but also craftsmen, to settle in its vicinity. It can be safely assumed that this factor, as well as the presence of the abbey, encouraged the growth of a lay settlement at the abbey's north gate. It was not unique for a small township to grow up beside a Scottish Cistercian house; Culross and Kinloss both emerged beside a Cistercian nucleus. According to local tradition, the Coupar people at this time were subject to the authority of the abbot through his regality court, said to have met on the mound at Beech Hill.[77]

There is indication that, from the fourteenth century, the monastery did not continue to prosper as it had initially. The evidence, however, would suggest that the abbey complex was not totally neglected as repair and maintenance work continued, if somewhat spasmodically. In 1320x28, for example, Maurice, bishop of Dunblane, agreed to the appropriation of the church of Fossoway 'because the monastery of Coupar ... through diverse hazards of wars and other chance occurrences will be very greatly bereft in its buildings and other things needful for divine worship and this life'.[78] Some thirty years later, Pope Clement VI granted the annexation of the church of Errol since the monastery was 'through diverse hazards of war, exceedingly impoverished in its buildings without and within and in other things necessary for divine worship and human life and irretrievably deprived of many of its accustomed revenues'.[79] In 1389, Coupar Angus was bemoaning the serious reduction of its income because of wars, which had left their buildings in ruins, and the numerous visitors which the monastery housed.[80] Further indications of dilapidation and inadequate revenues continued into the fifteenth century:[81] in 1408 Cîteaux granted a partial remission of dues, because of 'the lamentable desolation of the abbey of Coupar'.[82]

Coupar had been one of the abbeys responsible for helping to meet the cost of the annual chapter general at Cîteaux from *c* 1220, when Alexander II granted the church of Airlie to Coupar, on condition that it provided an annual pension to the Cistercian mother house.[83] Payments appear to have been transacted, albeit sometimes in arrears, until September 1329, when it was in debt for the three preceding years.[84] Over the next two decades, difficulties in meeting its obligation confirmed the views expressed by Maurice, bishop of Dunblane and Pope Clement VI, that Coupar was in straitened circumstances. Although the abbey attempted to meet its necessary dues, by 1408, as indicated, a remission was granted. The reduced annual payment, however, does not appear to have been paid as there is no mention of Coupar in the chapter's general accounts for 1403–28.[85] Forty years later, since many daughter houses were finding difficulties with regular payments and redemptions were being introduced, it was agreed that the pension on Airlie should cease on a final payment at Bruges at Christmas 1448. Although provision was made for the postponement of this transaction, Coupar paid it promptly, in the October.[86]

Whether this is an indication of a change of fortune is unclear. In 1429, the monastery had been sufficiently confident to appeal to Rome that its present abbot and successors should be entitled to wear mitre, ring and other pontifical insignia and be authorised to give solemn benedictions after masses, vespers and matins, because of its importance, wealth and daughter houses.[87] (In fact, Coupar had no daughter house; although a confirmation charter of Alexander II had ratified donations for two monks in a chapel on Forfar loch, there had been no further reference to this putative cell.[88]) The abbot was finally mitred in 1464.[89] There are distinct signs of an active monastic community in the early sixteenth century: building work was under way;[90] there were twenty-eight monks in 1521 and, still, twenty in 1558–9.[91] None of this suggests an establishment which was 'falling into decay', the final ruin of which was to be completed by 'a number of furious reformers from Perth', on the eve of the Reformation.[92]

It is uncertain whether there was an attack on the monastic buildings at this time. In 1563, a catalogue of repairs was recorded. These included the stacking of slates in the cloister, the repairing of the granaries and stables (which may have been situated at the abbey grange), the blocking of doorways to prevent access by looters to timber from the church and steeple, and the renewing of the abbot's windows which were 'all broken'.[93] If buildings had to be blockaded from looters, this would hint that not all held the abbey in high regard. However, there could not have been wholesale devastation: the abbey had still been a suitable abode for Queen Mary (1542–67) in 1562.[94] In 1685, Andrew, seventh earl of Errol was buried at the abbey beside his fifteen Hay ancestors,[95] which suggests that many of the old ways continued after the Reformation.

The last abbot, Donald Campbell, gave the five large estates of the monastery—Keithock, Arthurstone, Denhead, Balgersho and Cronon—to his five sons.[96] He also made lesser gifts of abbey possessions to other relatives immediately prior to the Reformation.[97] Whether under pressure or not, he quickly adapted to the reformed habits, agreeing to abolish the trappings of Catholicism and the mass.[98] In January 1563, Archibald Campbell, fifth earl of Argyll, was granted, during the queen's pleasure, half of all the income from mills, rentals and general profits of the abbey, along with half of the lands, kirks, mills, woods, fishings and emoluments belonging to it.[99] Two and a half years later, John, fourth earl of Atholl and brother-in-law of Donald Campbell, and his heirs were similarly favoured, until a new abbot was provided to the monastery, since the profits and emoluments of the abbey were 'now vacant'.[100] It is likely that Argyll had been dispossessed for his involvement in the abortive rebellion known as the 'Chase-about Raid', following Queen Mary's marriage to Lord Darnley.

The earls of Argyll were not to be permanently displaced, although controversy was rife over who should exercise jurisdiction over the abbey. In 1591, for example, the earl of Argyll and James, fifth Lord Ogilvie, were in dispute. The Ogilvie family had had close links with the abbey as James, fourth Lord Ogilvie of Airlie, had been created hereditary bailie of the regality of Coupar by Abbot Donald Campbell, which was confirmed in 1540. His brother, or nephew, Archibald Ogilvie of Lawtoun, was bailie-depute in 1563.[101] The Master of Ogilvie, son of the fifth Lord Ogilvie, believing that the dean of Brechin was supporting the Argyll cause, 'did take and ruffle the Deane with such disgrace' that a group of Argyll supporters killed fifteen or sixteen of Ogilvie's tenants.[102] In return, four Campbells living near the Master of Ogilvie were slain. Since these were Atholl's men, this brought the earl of Atholl potentially into the fray, with his offer of 4,000 men to avenge the slaughter.[103] In 1598, the tenants of the lordship of Coupar, weary of the constant feuding between Ogilvie and Atholl as to the bailie rights to Coupar, took them both to court.[104]

In 1563, after the death of Donald Campbell, Leonard Leslie was appointed as abbot-commendator by the earl of Atholl. He was deprived of his office sometime before 26 December 1595, to be replaced by George Halyburton and, in 1603, by James VI's chaplain, Andrew Lamb. Finally, on 24 January 1607, Lamb resigned his title and all the property and privileges which were associated with the post, in favour of James Elphinstone, second son of the first Lord Balmerino, since 'the convent of the said Abbey [was] all now deceased'.[105] An entry in the *Records of the Privy Council*, however, suggests that there was still an element of dispute over who had rights in Coupar: on 27 July 1607 Patrick Stirling, 'commendator of Coupar Angus Abbey' complained of molestation of himself by a number of parties, because of his possession of Coupar Abbey property, which he described as 'the monasterie, houssis, biggings, yairdis, archyairdis, medows and parkis'.[106] Whether Stirling was truly commendator at this date, the establishment in that same month of the burgh of Coupar under the superiority of James Elphinstone, second son of Lord Balmerino (*see below*), meant that jurisdiction over the former abbey's lands and tenants became more settled.

How much these events affected the people in the township of Coupar Angus is unclear. It has been suggested that the abbey church had already begun to function as the church for the local people;[107] they may also have been using the abbey graveyard as their burial ground. Possible children's graves, discovered during recent excavations, might support this theory.[108] The portioning out of abbey estates at a distance from the township probably made little impact on the lives of the local people; the dividing up of monastic lands in the township itself was more likely to have an effect. In 1573, for example, sasine was given on the outer yard of the monastery, which stood to the west of the outer gate, outwith the walls of the monastery.[109]

Eight years later, the customs of Coupar market were resigned to Alexander Leslie, son of Leonard Leslie, commendator of Coupar, by John Crago of Woulfhill (Wolfhill).[110] This information is important. It gives clear indication that the market continued to function after the Reformation. The old market cross still maintained its significant role, not only as the focal point for the market, but also as the place where important declarations of public interest were made. When Robert Portar, porter of the abbey, then 'old and decrepit', for example, resigned the office to his oldest son, David, along with its monk's portion, the chamber near the abbey gates and all the benefits which went with the office, it was ratified at the market cross.[111] The appearance of the name of Mr John Tully, schoolmaster of Coupar, twice in 1581 as witness to two charters of Leonard Leslie would suggest that other facets of community living were also continuing.[112]

Another charter of Leonard Leslie, also dated 1581, granted to his son, Alexander, lands in Boghall and Baitscheill, along with the privileges of the burgh of barony of Keithick; of greater significance for the emerging town of Coupar, it also referred to the same privileges 'of the tenants of Baitscheill and Calsayend'.[113] Clearly, there were already established two closely related settlements at Coupar, even if these suburbs would not have been intensively developed. When John Porter had been appointed as hereditary porter to the abbey, sometime between 1480 and 1509, he had been granted, amongst other things, a dwelling house at Baitscheill with six acres of arable land and pasturage for two horses and seven cows and their young, which suggests a particularly rural atmosphere.[114] Primary source material indicates, also, that close by Calsayend the 'treyn-mercat' (tree market) had already been established.[115]

It was this existing population that would form the nucleus of the burgh of barony of Coupar Angus. In 1607, the temporal lordship of James Elphinstone, second son of the first Lord Balmerino, created for him out of the remaining lands and baronies of the abbey (*see above*), was constituted a burgh of barony; Elphinstone received the title of Baron, or Lord, Coupar.[116]

There is an element of doubt about the status of the town of Coupar immediately prior to this date. The *Register of the Great Seal* refers to the 'villam' of Coupar being *de novo* erected into a burgh of barony.[117] The only evidence found to support this, to date, is a confirmation of a gift by commendator Leonard Leslie in 1580: it refers to a burgess of the burgh of Coupar Angus.[118] Had Coupar never been an abbot's burgh, this might seem unusual, but one of the main motivations for raising an existing township into a burgh, or creating one anew, was economic. The burgh superior would benefit from market dues. In the case of Coupar Angus, there was perhaps little incentive to such an elevation, as the abbots appear to have successfully continued to hold a market without burghal status. The nearby township of Keithick had been created a free burgh of barony as early as 1492.[119] The abbots probably saw little advantage in promoting the settlement at their gates.

the seventeenth century

From 1607, with burghal status, Lord Coupar had the right to appoint bailies, a treasurer and a dean of guild, as well as 'consules', which may be interpreted either as bailies or as members of a burgh council. Burgesses were to be made; and they were to have the right to trade freely, with markets and four three-day fairs. There was to be a tolbooth and a market cross, the secular focal points of the burgh. The new burgh superior was to have the right to grant out burgh lands, hold courts and dispense justice and punishments in his burgh.[120] Clearly, there was to be little self-determination for the new burgesses; but they would benefit from the continuing market, as would the burgh superior who stood to gain financially from the dues imposed at both market and fair.

Lack of burgh records for this period leaves it unclear whether there was, at this point, a formal allocation of lands—burgage plots or tofts—to the new burgesses, who might have been incomers as well as natives of Coupar Angus. It would have been in Lord Coupar's interest to encourage a strong, economically viable sub-structure to his new burgh and this could have been attained by the offer of burghal privileges and property. This makes it likely that the population rose during the first decades of the seventeenth century. Incomers would have required land on which to build their dwellings; probably these plots or tofts were measured out by burghal officers called 'liners'. Whether the existing population was affected by a reallocation of lands is uncertain.

A market cross already existed, and its position within the town setting and Coupar's street pattern is interesting. Unlike the majority of Scottish medieval and early modern towns, which had an axial main street with back lanes running parallel and burgage plots set in herring-bone pattern from the main street, Coupar's streets radiate out from a central point, The Cross **figure 15**. This probably evolved at the intersection of important thoroughfares—from Perth, Dundee and from the north via the ferry-boat crossing or the fording point across the Isla. Until recent years, the flood stone that indicated water level at the ford was visible; to this day, in the dry season, the causey stones of the ford are clearly visible a little to the east of Bendochy Church.[121] It was probably via this route that the abbots had passed to one of their two country seats—Coupar Grange. The route to Dundee, on the other hand, could not originally have been aligned as at present, as the abbey complex occupied an area that encompassed the present Dundee Road; and the current road to Perth, George Street, is a modern development, as is Union Street. Calton Street was the original main east–west thoroughfare. These routeways converged on the focal point of the settlement at the now defunct abbey gates—the market cross.

The market appears to have continued to function without hiatus. The customs or tolls were imposed regularly; and a reference to the customs of Coupar's markets (plural) suggests an element of specialisation.[122] A 'trein mercat' or timber market existed in Coupar from at least the sixteenth century and was still functioning in 1605.[123] On 28 November 1616, John Forrester, bailie, held the court of the 'land and lordship of Coupar'. It was laid down that any fleshers who brought decaying meat to the market at Coupar would be brought to court and fined £5, which might imply a specific meat market; although the fleshers could merely have been attending the general market,[124] which was held weekly, on Fridays at this time.[125]

The tolbooth was the building where dues, or tolls, to use the market were collected. There is no mention in the records of a medieval tolbooth, but in 1607 Lord Coupar was given the right to erect one. How soon this was achieved is uncertain. There is a reference in the *Records of the Privy Council* in 1619 to the tolbooth, market cross and stocks of Coupar; but, although indexed as 'Coupar Angus', the text refers merely to 'Couper' and there may be a confusion with Cupar in Fife.[126] Two years later, however, in the same source there is mention of Lord Ogilvie of Airlie, bailie principal of the Lordship of Coupar, and his deputies holding courts in the tolbooth of the burgh.[127]

Coupar was clearly functioning as a well-established small burgh, although the respective roles in the town of Lord Coupar, as burgh superior, and Lord Ogilvie, as hereditary bailie of the lordship of Coupar, might at times lead to an element of confusion. In 1625, for example, there was a dispute between the two as to who was responsible for overseeing the regular musters. It was decided that neither would be in charge, the honour being given to one of the sheriff deputes in Perth.[128]

Documentary evidence indicates that Coupar's corn mill, on Coupar Burn, established long previously by the abbey, continued to function. In 1610, James, earl of Atholl, disponed to James Drummond in Boghall certain lands at Coupar, which included the corn mill. Drummond would have been expecting a return on his substantial investment of 10,000 merks; part of this would have come from payments from the townspeople for use of the mill.[129]

Lord Coupar appears to have maintained his household on abbey property and possibly the abbot's quarters would have been the most suitable.[130] This is also further evidence that the supposed destruction at the Reformation has been highly exaggerated (*see* p 22). The Protestant minister lived in the town, in a dwelling house with a yard. In 1635, Lord Coupar entered into an agreement with the minister, Mr Robert Lindsay, that four and a half acres would be set aside for a manse and a glebe; but until all was ready, the minister would continue to live in his house in Coupar.[131]

This arrangement was a somewhat belated consequence of an obligation entered into by Lord Coupar in 1618. In that year, James VI (1567–1625) confirmed the lordship of Coupar. At the special request of the king, Lord Coupar agreed that, as the parish of Bendochy was divided by the Water of Isla and as it was sometimes dangerous for those parishioners south of the river to attend the parish church at Bendochy, he would build a new kirk within the precincts of the monastery, to be called the kirk of Coupar, to serve as parish church for Coupar and the parish of Bendochy south of the Isla. He also agreed to provide the minister with a manse, glebe and a stipend of 500 merks; in return he would have the hereditary right of patronage to the new parish church.[132] The fact that he agreed to build a new church suggests that the abbey church was, by this time, beyond repair.

There is no evidence as to whether Robert Lindsay enjoyed the new manse promised to him in 1635. Ten years later, he was dead. Lord Coupar was a supporter of the Covenanters; and, in April 1645, 200 men of James Graham, marquis of Montrose, led by Sir Alexander Macdonald and Forbes of Skellater, descended on Coupar Angus, with the intention of teaching Lord Coupar a lesson. He was not at home. The minister and others were killed, the town was 'fyrit' and the residence of Lord Coupar was attacked.[133] How great an effect this had on the material fabric of the town is not documented. As the town was burnt, many buildings would have had to be repaired or even replaced. The abbey structures, whether in ruins or still partially standing, may have been useful quarries. Many of the town's domestic buildings to this day reveal that they were partially or entirely built of erstwhile abbey stone **figure 10**.[134]

figure 10
Ruins of
Coupar Angus Abbey
© Crown Copyright:
RCAHMS

The available evidence seems to suggest that Lord Coupar permitted his residence to fall into disrepair after the 1645 attack. How much damage was done is not clear, although it is known that it was 'spoiled and plundered'.[135] He was fined £3,000 by the Cromwellian regime in 1654, although this was later reduced to £750; and £4,800 by the Restoration government for failure to support episcopacy.[136] Whether this caused financial embarrassment is unclear; but his nephew, John, third Lord Balmerino, who succeeded him in 1669, felt it necessary to charge Lord Coupar's widow 'to repair and put in order the manor place of Coupar'.[137] Little seems to have been achieved. In the mid 1680s it was described as having been 'a very sweet place ... in very pleasant countryside' but 'now nothing but rubbish'.[138]

It does not seem that Lord Coupar fulfilled his promise to erect a new parish church for the residents south of the Isla. In 1683, the bishop of Dunkeld set up a commission of ministers, wrights and masons to inspect the kirk of Coupar. They declared that it was 'quite ruinous' and 'altogether unsafe to come to hear sermon in it'. They estimated that it would cost six times as much to repair as it would to put up a new building in the churchyard.[139] From April 1683, because of the state of the kirk's fabric, services were to be held in 'the low vaults of the abbay'.[140] During that year a number of improvements were effected to this 'laigh abbey': a pulpit and reader's seat were moved in; doors were added and some masonry work done; glass was put in the window at the gable where the pulpit stood and another little window was glazed.[141] Although it is clear that some repair work had to be done to make the vault adequately comfortable for worship, the state of the 'laigh abbey' was, at least, relatively wind and water-tight; this suggests, yet again, that Reformation damage has been exaggerated. In 1685, Mr George Hay, minister, complained to Lord Balmerino that Lord Coupar had, instead of building a church, merely allotted one of his own 'ruinous office-houses which was above the gate' and that it 'was dangerous to be in'. The heritors were instructed to build a new one, 'in the abbey cemetery', and also a school house, above the former prison.[142]

Most of the heritors appeared willing to oblige and stented themselves at £28 per £100 of valued rent.[143] This was a high rate, which bore rewards. Three masons (Alexander Rae, Patrick Brown and William Archer) started work in May 1686. They were to begin by digging the foundations, with the help of two barrowmen; one James Simson junior was to demolish the walls of the old church; John Barclay was to carry the stones to the new site; and James Gourlay was to dig and carry the mortar.[144] By the following December, the minister reported that since 'the fabrick and rooff' of the new church were now complete worship would commence there.[145] The following Sunday, the bishop of Aberdeen preached in the new kirk.[146]

Further embellishments of the church continued, including rich trappings for the pulpit, a lectern and collection boards.[147] The minister also suggested that as the heritors had provided the townspeople with sufficient seats in the middle of the church at no cost to themselves, there should be a collection for silver communion plate and tablecloths. All but £11 8s of the cost of two new communion cups was raised. These were made at Perth, weighed twenty-seven ounces and cost £102 12s.[148] This was a huge sum of money to be raised by the inhabitants of a small town; it is indicative not only of affection for the church, but also of considerable wealth in the community. The communion cups survive to this day.

Some carvings from the original abbey church were moved into the new building; in spite of post seventeenth-century rebuilding of the church (*see* p 30) these may still be viewed. The tomb slab of Abbot John Schanwel, who died in 1506, and the effigy of Sir Thomas Hay of Errol, third Hay constable of Scotland, are extant in Coupar Angus parish church. They had been buried here because of their prestigious positions. The parish church of Bendochy had been the traditional burial ground before the parish was split. Two of the five sons of Abbot Donald Campbell, David Campbell of Denhead and Nicoll Campbell of Keithock, were buried in the parish church of Bendochy, where a mural monument commemorates them; and the first lay commendator, Leonard Leslie, is likewise honoured.

Although it is not possible to recreate a complete town plan, the little available documentary evidence suggests that, by the latter half of the seventeenth century, a number of streets led to or stood near the market cross. There were at least three streets to the east of the cross, which may have been cobbled, since they are referred to as 'causeys'. Another street was called 'Market Wynd'. The fact that a tenement of land, named 'the outsteid', on this street had a croft of land to its north is clear indication that there was little congestion in the market centre. To the west of this tenement and croft, a routeway called the 'Stripe' led to Causewayend (Calseyend); and the 'Common hie way' to Causewayend lay to its east.[149] This road had houses, a barn, a malt-house and a kiln, at least, on its west frontage. West of the market place was the timber market. This, too, was bounded on its north by tenements and at least one croft. Between the timber market and market place there were tenements and other buildings,[150] including a carpenter's premises and 'shopmanstandes', which were presumably the booths of the local merchants and craftsmen.[151]

The Register of Baptisms indicates that settlement was not solely concentrated around the market place, focal point of the town though this was. It is unclear how far the settlement pattern at Beitchhill (Baitscheill; Beech Hill) and Causewayend had extended over the previous hundred years, but the number of births would suggest significant little suburbs. Another interesting suburb to the original market nucleus was 'the Precinct'. Clearly, with the destruction of much of the abbey complex, there had been colonisation in the abbey precincts, probably near to the present Precinct Street.[152] There was also settlement in Lay Lyes, Meadow Lyes and Long Leis,[153] Dykehead,[154] Bogside[155] and 'the boat',[156] which was probably near the present Boatlands.

These records also give an impression of the occupations of some of the Coupar inhabitants. They included fleshers, fishmongers, brewers, bakers, weavers, dyers, glaziers, carpenters, tilers, masons, glovers, tailors, skinners, shoemakers, candlemakers, 'tobaccomen', as well as writers, kirk officers, bailies, the schoolmaster and the clerk to the regality court of Coupar.[157]

It is difficult to quantify the population size at this time. An assessment of the number of hearths for the purposes of taxation, in 1694, considered the parish as a whole. There were only 313 hearths in the whole parish, which was 5.6 by 1.6 km in extent. This does not suggest intensive settlement. There are specific references to few properties in the town itself. The clerk of Coupar had a house with five hearths; only six other properties are noted, one of which had five hearths, one with four, two with three and two with two. In the parish as a whole, there were only two properties with single hearths, which is distinctly unusual in small towns, and might appear to indicate that the properties were relatively substantial. Most of them seem, however, to have housed more than one family.[158]

This same source also lists the poor of the parish. There are only three names. This figure does not tally with information in the contemporary kirk session register. It suggests that not only was there a considerable number of poor and beggars in the district but also that the Coupar Angus parishioners were generous with their funds. In April 1690, for example, £2 8s was given to the common poor who came to the church door, as well as £4 16s to the poor of their own parish.[159] This generosity may have been abused. In the autumn of that year, there was such an influx of strangers into the town that the session ordained that certificates should be produced to prove entitlement.[160] Fifteen months later, the number of poor supported by the church doubled, perhaps because of extremely foul weather.[161] The church authorities continued to be liberal in their support, but the poor were not a problem that would go away. In March 1695, the minister warned from the pulpit that anyone found supporting fugitives or other vagrants who did not have a certificate, especially women with child, would be pursued by both the civil and ecclesiastical authorities.[162] Whether this was a reflection of famine in the area is unclear; but it was certainly an attempt to discourage the high level of pregnancies outwith marriage that is recorded. In June of the following year, the number of licensed poor increased again because of a 'great dearth in the land'.[163] The burden on the townspeople was exacerbated in the following winter and spring, when troops were quartered in the town.[164] The records from the August of 1698 until October 1699 are missing but, when they recommence, the parish church is found distributing all of the collection money every Sabbath to the poor, other than two shillings retained for the beadle.[165] In spite of these efforts, by 1700 there were reports of the poor starving; the problem remained an on-going one for Coupar Angus, as for other urban centres, well into the eighteenth century.[166]

the eighteenth and nineteenth centuries

Little else seems to have disturbed Coupar's peace in the early decades of the eighteenth century. There are varying local traditions as to the age of the Cumberland Barracks (*see above*) **figure 11**: one view is that it was in existence in the seventeenth century at the time of the Covenanting wars; another is that it was constructed in the early eighteenth century, as a base for anti-Jacobite activities. Certainly, Coupar was ideally placed on a main routeway northwards to the Highlands, and proved to be a convenient resting spot for Hanoverian troops en route. There were, also, troops billeted in the town in the last decade of the seventeenth century (*see above*). The extant records, however, give no indication of unrest or unease at the time of the 1707 Union or at the 'Fifteen Rebellion. John, fourth Lord Balmerino joined the Jacobite cause, but later received a pardon.[167]

Whatever its origins, the Cumberland Barracks was fully functional by the time of the 'Forty–Five campaign. It was named after the duke of Cumberland who led the government forces in Scotland against Prince Charles Edward Stuart. Coupar was at the south end of two roads forged through the countryside for rapid movement of troops and efficient supplying of remote government garrisons. The main routeway led via Blairgowrie and Braemar to Fort George on the Moray Firth. Cumberland Barracks was the last stopping point in the Lowlands for many Hanoverian soldiers. Attitudes to the Jacobites varied in the town. Lord Balmerino, again, was a faithful supporter, fighting at the Battle of Culloden. He was taken prisoner, tried in London and beheaded on Tower Hill.[168] The members of the kirk session were less enamoured of the Jacobite cause; its register recorded in September 1745 that the 'apprehending of delinquents [was] weakened by the landing of the Pretender's eldest son and a great number of the Highland Clans gathering to him, two hundred whereof came to Coupar ... under the command of Alexander McDonald of Capoch'.[169] In the following December, they still bemoaned that their country was 'in great confusion by continual harassing and ravagings of the rebel Highlanders'.[170]

figure 11
Rear of Cumberland Barracks 1995

figure 12
The Defiance Inn, now the Royal Hotel, in the late nineteenth century

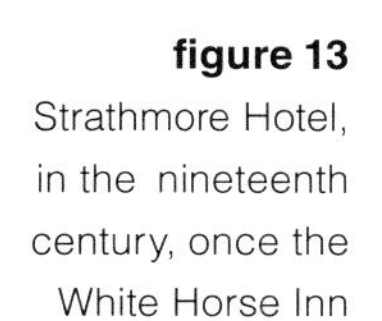

figure 13
Strathmore Hotel, in the nineteenth century, once the White Horse Inn

Building work in the town during this century, however, attests to more generally peaceful times. The church was a continuing commitment, as were the manse and the schoolhouse.[171] There were almost constant repairs to the church fabric, and in 1715 a new bellhouse was built for it, with the bell being brought from Dundee.[172] Some standing buildings are still reminders of Coupar's past (*see* pp 59–63). The Masonic Hall in Gray Street, once used partly as a school, is a fine example of quality building. The Royal Hotel, originally called the Defiance Inn, took its first name from the stage-coach that stopped there daily on the Edinburgh–Perth–Aberdeen run **figure 12**. Across the road, the White House or White Horse Inn, now the Strathmore Hotel, was also a hostelry for travellers **figure 13**.[173] At the rear, a few remnants of the stables and tethering rings for the use of visitors' horses are still visible. Visitors to Coupar were to find their journeys much improved after 1766 with the construction of Couttie Bridge across the Isla. Many had

figure 14
Level crossing, High Street, also showing The Steeple, in the early twentieth century

until then been forced to use the boat at Croonan, linking the route between Alyth and Coupar.[174] A further improvement for transport was projected in the 1760s, when George Young, a linen manufacturer in the town, had a survey prepared with the intention of linking Perth and Forfar by canal. In the event, the scheme, which would have assisted Coupar's growing manufacturing interests, was abandoned.[175]

A number of eighteenth-century houses, or remnants of them, are indication that Coupar was a modestly wealthy, small country town (*see* pp 60–1). The Steeple, or tolbooth tower, was built by public subscription in 1762 and completed in 1769 **figure 14**. It is purportedly on the site of the former High Court of Justiciary. The Steeple was to serve as a gaol on the ground floor and as a meeting house for local courts on the upper floors. Until the Steeple was erected, regality courts and the bailie court had been held in the open air, at Beech Hill. Although a partial ruin, much of the original of the Steeple remains. It, as with other architecture in the town, is a comment on the substance of the townspeople. Coupar was not a large town and the construction of the Steeple must have been a major public undertaking.

The parish also considered itself to have sufficient resources to substantially rebuild the church in the 1780s. It was at this time that one of the remaining parts of the old abbey was removed—'an arch, of beautiful architecture, situate near the centre of the ... churchyard, was demolished for the purpose of furnishing stones for the ... church'.[176] A visitor in the 1790s noted the vestiges of the abbey still standing, but whether there was visibly more than what remains today is unclear.[177] By the 1790s there was also an Antiburgher church and a Relief meeting house in the town. The manse was rebuilt in 1781 and the school, which was 'large and well-lighted' and averaged sixty scholars, in 1792.[178] Other than the Steeple, it is not clear how much of the funds to make these improvements came from the town itself and how much came from the parish. There were wealthy landowners in the area. The head court roll of the Lordship and Regality of Coupar Angus of 1747, for example, listed eighty-two names: only five were given as being specifically from Coupar; two were dukes (Atholl and Argyll) and three were earls (Perth, Strathmore and Breadalbane).[179]

There had been a considerable increase in the population during the eighteenth century, largely as a result of linen manufacture. Much of this was attributed to George Young, the merchant and linen manufacturer who pressurised for the building of the canal.[180] Earlier evidence dating from the 1730s and 1740s, however, suggests that there was already by then a gradually increasing number of merchants in the town, a number of vintners and at least one surgeon.[181] From a parish population of 1,491 in 1755, the figure rose to 2,076 by 1793. 1,604 people lived in the town itself in 520 families.[182] One

figure 15
The Cross, looking down George Street, in the early twentieth century

visitor in 1760 had described Coupar as 'a poor small town, in which they have a little manufactory of linnen'.[183] Coupar had a small spinning school by 1763. In 1792, approximately 98,000 yards of brown linen and 117,000 of yarn were stamped and sold to England from the town and parish. Some of the yarn came from Dundee, where the flax, imported from the Baltic, was spun. It was then sent on to Alyth and other towns as well as Coupar.[184] The finished linen, which was used for buckram, was worth about 9d a yard, and harn, being coarser, 5d. The town also had a tannery, built in 1781, which dressed about 2,600 hides annually. There were four distilleries in the parish also offering employment, three being of forty-gallon capacity and one of thirty. The town continued to hold a weekly market, now on Thursdays, and there were four fairs annually—in April, May, July and December—as well as regular hiring fairs, where local agricultural labourers obtained seasonal work.[185]

Coupar's contacts with the rest of Scotland were much easier after the opening of the railway in 1837. The Newtyle and Coupar Angus Railway Company had been incorporated in 1835, employing the local surveyor, William Blackadder. Although its seal depicts a locomotive surrounded with the symbols of speed and time and carries the motto 'Time is Precious', the service was horse-drawn for much of the time until it was incorporated in 1847 into the Dundee, Perth and Aberdeen Railway Junction Company.[186] The railway was to have an impact not only on the life of the Coupar people, but also on the townscape. The line cut straight across the top of the High Street, where level crossing gates operated **figure 14.**

Many other changes were to be made to the townscape. New access roads—George Street to the west leading to Perth and Union Street to the east of The Cross **figure 15**—relieved some of the congestion in the old main thoroughfare, Calton Street. A new hotel was erected beside the railway station—the Railway Hotel, now called the Red House Hotel. The original inn had six rooms to let, a dining room and a bar for the comfort of passengers. Perhaps one of the most important innovations to the townspeople was the introduction of a municipal water supply in 1874. The Coupar Burn, increasingly foul, and numerous wells had been the sole supply. A local newspaper maintained that the state of the burn was such that in it 'numerous cats and dogs suffering from senile decay usually terminated their existence, so that the water may have resembled clear soup in flavour'.[187] A number of the old wells remain in back gardens in the town, many of them infilled for safety. Also still standing are a number of buildings which give a feel of nineteenth-century Coupar Angus (*see* pp 61–3). The eighteenth-century restored church was replaced by the present Victorian church in 1859, built to the design of local architect John Carver **figure 18**. By 1886, there were a number of other churches, including the Free Church, United Presbyterian, Evangelical Union, Original Secession and the Episcopalians.[188] A new school had also been built in 1876–7 with accommodation for 502 children; and there were two other unendowed schools.[189] In 1887, the Town Hall, a symbol of civic pride, was built at a cost of £4,000, to celebrate Queen Victoria's jubilee **figure 20**.

By the late nineteenth century the town had three linen works, a tannery, farina works, a brewery and steam sawmills. A waulk mill stood to the north of Precinct Street. Water, fed by a lade from the Coupar Burn to the south-east, was controlled by sluice gates. After leaving the mill it led, in an open lade, back into the Coupar Burn to the north **figure 25**. There were weekly grain markets on Thursdays, which brought in the local farming population, and cattle fairs in September and October.[190] Coupar was also renowned for its annual horse market. Although it petered out in the 1920s, it was recalled for years in the gingerbread horses made by local bakers. Coupar was a small, but prosperous country town, relying on its local manufacturing, but still attracting the agricultural hinterland. In 1886, it was described as 'dating from a remote antiquity, the town was long a time-worn, decayed, and stagnant place, but within recent years has undergone great revival and improvement, and become a centre of much traffic and a seat of considerable trade'.[191]

notes

1 T Darvill, *Prehistoric Britain* (London, 1987), 63–4.
2 Royal Commission on the Ancient and Historical Monuments of Scotland, *South-East Perth: an Archaeological Landscape* (Edinburgh, 1994), 24–6; G J Barclay, G S Maxwell, I A Simpson & D A Davidson, 'The Cleaven Dyke: a Neolithic cursus monument/bank barrow in Tayside Region, Scotland', *Antiquity*, vol 69, no 263 (June 1995), 317–26.
3 Darvill, *Prehistoric Britain*, 75.
4 S Stevenson, 'The excavation of a kerbed cairn at Beech Hill House, Coupar Angus, Perthshire', *PSAS* 125 (1995), 197–236.
5 Darvill, *Prehistoric Britain*, 103.
6 RCAHMS, *South-East Perth*, 41–75.
7 *Ibid*, 55–7.
8 *Ibid*, 76.
9 L Keppie, *Scotland's Roman Remains* (Edinburgh, 1986), 8.
10 W Hanson & G Maxwell, *Rome's North-West Frontier: The Antonine Wall* (Edinburgh, 1983), 39.
11 Keppie, *Scotland's Roman Remains*, 11.
12 Hanson & Maxwell, *Rome's North-West Frontier*, 43.
13 Keppie, *Scotland's Roman Remains*, 16.
14 *Ibid*, 16.
15 *Ibid*, 18.
16 RCAHMS, *South-East Perth*, 76–7.
17 *Ibid*, 84.
18 *Ibid*, 86.
19 Walker & Ritchie, *Fife and Tayside*, 131.
20 *Ibid*, 131–2.
21 *RRS*, i, 42.
22 A J Warden, 'Parish of Coupar Angus', in *Angus or Forfarshire—the Land and People* (Edinburgh, 1881), 129.
23 *Rental*, i, pp v–vi.
24 *Charters*, i, p vi.
25 We are indebted to Professor G W S Barrow for his views on the origin of the name of Coupar.
26 Cowan & Easson, 73.
27 *Ibid*, 72.
28 *RRS*, i, 266.
29 RCAHMS, *South-East Perth*, 127.
30 Cf *Charters*, i, 33.
31 *Charters*, i, p xxiv.
32 I Alfonso, 'Cistercians and feudalism', *Past and Present*, cxxxiii (1991), 8.
33 R A Donkin, *Cistercian Studies in the Geography of England and Wales* (Toronto, 1988), 39.
34 *Ibid*, 40.
35 T B Franklin, *A History of Scottish Farming* (Edinburgh, 1952), 51–2.
36 Jocelyn, 'Life of Waltheof', *Acta Sanctorum Bollandi, August*, i, 248–77. We are indebted to Professor G W S Barrow for this reference.
37 *RRS*, i, no 226.
38 *RRS*, ii, no 154.
39 *RRS*, ii, nos 11–12.
40 *Charters*, i, p xxviii.
41 *RRS*, ii, no 414.
42 *Rental*, i, 331.
43 Cowan & Easson, 73.
44 P Courtney, 'Excavations in the outer precinct of Tintern Abbey', *Medieval Archaeology*, xxxiii (1989), 102.

45 *Rental*, ii, p xii.
46 G Coppack, 'The excavation of an outer court building, perhaps the wool-house, at Fountains Abbey, North Yorkshire', *Medieval Archaeology*, xxx (1989), 46–87.
47 *Rental*, i, p vi.
48 *Rental*, ii, 211.
49 *Ibid*, ii, 210.
50 *Charters*, ii, 213.
51 *Ibid*, ii, 237.
52 *Ibid*, ii, 293.
53 *Ibid*, ii, 249.
54 *RMS*, i, Appendix ii, no 1296, for example.
55 *Charters*, *passim*.
56 J O'Sullivan, 'Abbey, market and cemetery: topographical notes on Coupar Angus in Perthshire, with a description of archaeological excavations on glebe land by the parish church', *PSAS* 125 (1995), 1045–68.
57 RCAHMS, *South-East Perth*, 127.
58 National Register of Archives (Scotland), Inventory of the Moray Muniments, vol x, box no 32, division v, no 84 (November 1481), notarial instrument regarding rights of Coupar Abbey to certain tenements in Dundee.
59 E P D Torrie, *Medieval Dundee. A Town and its People* (Abertay Historical Society, 1990), 49.
60 *Rental*, i, 364–6.
61 Handlist of documents of Alexander II, SRO, Open shelf, 408.02.
62 *RMS*, i, no 663.
63 *RRS*, v, nos 110, 111.
64 *RRS*, vi, no 27.
65 *Charters*, i, p xx.
66 *RRS*, i, no 222; *RRS*, ii, no 509.
67 *RRS*, vi, no 121.
68 Dundee District Archive and Record Centre, CC1, no 17.
69 Torrie, *Medieval Dundee*, 31–3.
70 R K Hannay (ed), *Rentale Dunkeldense, being Accounts of the Bishopric (AD 1505–1517), with Myln's 'Lives of the bishops' (AD 1483–1517)* (SHS,1915), 12.
71 *TA*, ii, 425.
72 *Charters*, ii, 241.
73 *Ibid*, ii, 241.
74 *Rental*, i, 353–4.
75 *Ibid*, i, 353–4.
76 O'Sullivan, 'Abbey, market and cemetery'.
77 Warden, 'Parish of Coupar Angus', 134.
78 *Charters*, i, 222–3.
79 *Ibid*, i, 244–6.
80 C Burns (ed), *Calendar of Papal Letters to Scotland of Clement VII of Avignon, 1378–1394* (SHS, 1976), 80; 147–8.
81 *Charters*, ii, 1–2, 5–6, 7–8.
82 *Ibid*, ii, 10–11.
83 P King, 'Coupar Angus and Cîteaux', *Innes Review*, xxvii (1976), 50–1.
84 *Ibid*, 53.
85 *Ibid*, 55.
86 *Ibid*, 56.
87 A I Dunlop & I B Cowan (edd), *Calendar of Scottish Supplications to Rome, 1428–32* (SHS, 1970), 56.
88 *Charters*, i, p lxviii.
89 Cowan & Easson, 73.
90 *Ibid*, 73.
91 M Dilworth, 'Monks and ministers after 1560', *Records of the Scottish Church History Society*, xviii (1974), 207.
92 *OSA*, xi, 95–6.
93 *Rental*, ii, 280.
94 *Extracts from the Records of the Burgh of Edinburgh, AD 1557–1571* (SBRS, 1875), 148–9.
95 Warden, 'Parish of Coupar Angus', 130.
96 *Ibid*, 132.
97 *Rental*, ii, pp xxxii–iii.
98 *Charters*, ii, 190.
99 *RSS*, v, no 1199.
100 *Ibid*, v, no 2229; for further details of the income of the abbey at the time of the Reformation *see* J Kirk (ed), *The Books of Assumption of the Thirds of Benefices. Scottish Ecclesiastical Rentals at the Reformation* (Oxford, 1995), 282, 303, 332, 352–64, 368–71, 409–12, 509.
101 *Rental*, i, p xxxiv.
102 *RPC*, iv, nos 682–4; 777.
103 *CSP Scot*, x, 567.
104 SRO, GD 16/41/108, Airlie Muniments. Quoted in K M Brown, *Bloodfeud in Scotland, 1573–1625* (Edinburgh, 1986), 73.
105 *Charters*, ii, 251.
106 *RPC*, xiii, 533–4.

107 Cowan & Easson, 190.
108 O'Sullivan, 'Abbey, market and cemetery', 37.
109 NRAS, 217, Moray Muniments, Box 32, Division iv, Bundle v, no 104, instrument of sasine, February 1573.
110 *Ibid*, Bundle x, no 296.
111 *Rental*, ii, 293.
112 *Charters*, ii, 240–1.
113 *Ibid*, ii, 241.
114 *Rental*, ii, p xxviii.
115 *RMS*, vi, no 285.
116 *APS*, iv, 340.
117 *RMS*, vi, no 2002.
118 *RSS*, vii, no 2600.
119 *Charters*, ii, 96–8.
120 *RMS*, vi, no 2002.
121 We are indebted to Mrs Margaret Laing and Mr Pitkeathly for their assistance in locating the ford. Documentary evidence is singularly lacking for this period of Coupar's history. Five of the many protocol books in SRO, which might contain information on the Coupar area, were consulted, with little reward. These were NP1/86, Patrick Gourlaws, 1637–1664; NP1/161 Wm Henderson, 1667–late 1680s; NP1/16 Duncan Gray, 1554–1572; NP1/43 R Brown, 1584–1607; and NP1/72 A Keltie, 1620–31.
122 W Fraser (ed), *The Elphinstone Family Book of the Lords Elphinstone, Balmerino and Coupar*, 2 vols (Edinburgh, 1897), 264–7 includes the testament of James, first Lord Balmerino, 27 April 1612, which includes the customs of the markets of Coupar.
123 *RMS*, vi, no 1560.
124 SRO, GD 16/36/27, Airlie Muniments, 28 November 1616.
125 *APS*, iv, 498; *RPC*, viii, 213.
126 *RPC*, xii, 14.
127 *Ibid*, xii, 510–11.
128 *RPC*, i, 214.
129 *Rental*, ii, 304.
130 J Spalding, *The History of the Troubles and Memorable Transactions in Scotland and England from MDCXXIV to MDCXLV (1624–1645)*, 2 vols (Bannatyne Club, 1829), ii, 315.
131 SRO, TE5/218, Teind Records.
132 *RMS*, vii, no 1956.
133 Spalding, *History of the Troubles*, ii, 315.
134 T McGibbon & D Ross, *The Ecclesiastical Architecture of Scotland*, 3 vols (Edinburgh, 1897), iii, 492.
135 *APS*, vi, part ii, 338–9.
136 *Rental*, i, p liii.
137 SRO, NRAS Darnaway, 217, Box 32/292.
138 W Macfarlane, 'Geographical description of severall parishes in Perthshire, 1st of the paroch of Alyth' in *Geographical Collections Relating to Scotland*, ed A Mitchell (3 vols) (SHS, 1906–8), ii, 35; J Maidment (ed), *The Spottiswoode Miscellany*, 2 vols (Edinburgh, 1844–5), i, 332.
139 SRO CH2/395/1, Coupar Angus Kirk Session Records, 1682–1703, 4 February 1683.
140 *Ibid*, 1 April 1683.
141 *Ibid*, 8 April 1683; 15 September 1683; 7 October 1683.
142 *RPC*, Third Series, i, 54–5.
143 SRO CH2/395/1, 18 April 1686.
144 *Ibid*, 9 May 1686.
145 *Ibid*, 12 [*sic*, correct date was 5] December 1686.
146 *Ibid*, 12 December 1686.
147 *Ibid*, 20 March 1687.
148 *Ibid*, 29 May 1687; 8 August 1687.
149 *RMS*, xi, no 607.
150 *Ibid*, xi, no 631.
151 *Ibid*, xi, no 1004.
152 SRO CH2/395/1, eg 12 April 1688.
153 *Ibid*, eg 2 September 1689.
154 *Ibid*, eg 23 April 1688.
155 *Ibid*, eg 18 January 1691.
156 *Ibid*, eg 7 May 1690.
157 *Ibid*, *passim*.
158 SRO E69/19/2, Hearth Tax, Presbyteries of Perth and Dunkeld.
159 SRO CH2/395/1, 27 April 1690.
160 *Ibid*, September, October 1690.
161 *Ibid*, 31 January 1692.
162 *Ibid*, [nn] March 1695.
163 *Ibid*, 21 & 30 June 1696.
164 *Ibid*, autumn 1696, spring 1697, *passim*.
165 *Ibid*, 29 October 1699.
166 SRO CH2/395/2, Co upar Angus Kirk Session Records, 1703–24, which includes the Register of Disciplinary Proceedings of the Church Session of Coupar,

together with a monthly and annual Account of the Poor's Money.

167 Warden, 'Parish of Coupar Angus', 132.

168 *Ibid*, 132.

169 SRO CH2/395/4, Coupar Angus Kirk Session Records, 1726–47, 1 September 1745.

170 *Ibid*, 29 December 1745.

171 SRO CH2/395/2, 28 November 1700.

172 *Ibid*, 1715, *passim*.

173 M Laing (ed), *Coupar Angus Newsletter* (Coupar Angus, 1994), no 41, unpaginated.

174 *Geographical Collections*, i, 111.

175 *OSA*, xi, 91.

176 *NSA*, x, 1144.

177 R Heron, *Scotland Delineated* (Edinburgh, 1975; orig pub 1799), 129–30.

178 *OSA*, xi, 94.

179 SRO GD 16/36/29, Head Court Roll of the Lordship and Regality of Coupar Angus, 1747.

180 *OSA*, xi, 90.

181 SRO GD 16/36/25, Minute Book of the Inhibitions, Hornings etc., Registered in the Particular Register of the Regality of Coupar Angus, 1731–46.

182 *OSA*, xi, 90, 92.

183 R Pococke, *Tours in Scotland 1747, 1750, 1760*, ed D W Kemp (SHS, 1887), 224–5.

184 J A R Macdonald, *The History of Blairgowrie* (Blairgowrie, 1899), 166.

185 *OSA*, xi, 91.

186 C H Dingwall, *Ardler—A Village History. The Planned Railway Village of Washington* (Abertay Historical Society, 1985), 21.

187 *Perthshire Advertiser*, Centenary Number, Special Edition, 1929.

188 F H Groome, *Ordnance Gazetteer of Scotland: A Survey of Scottish Topography*, 6 vols (Edinburgh, 1886), ii, 290.

189 *NSA*, x, 1148.

190 Groome, *Gazetteer*, ii, 290.

191 *Ibid*, ii, 289–90.

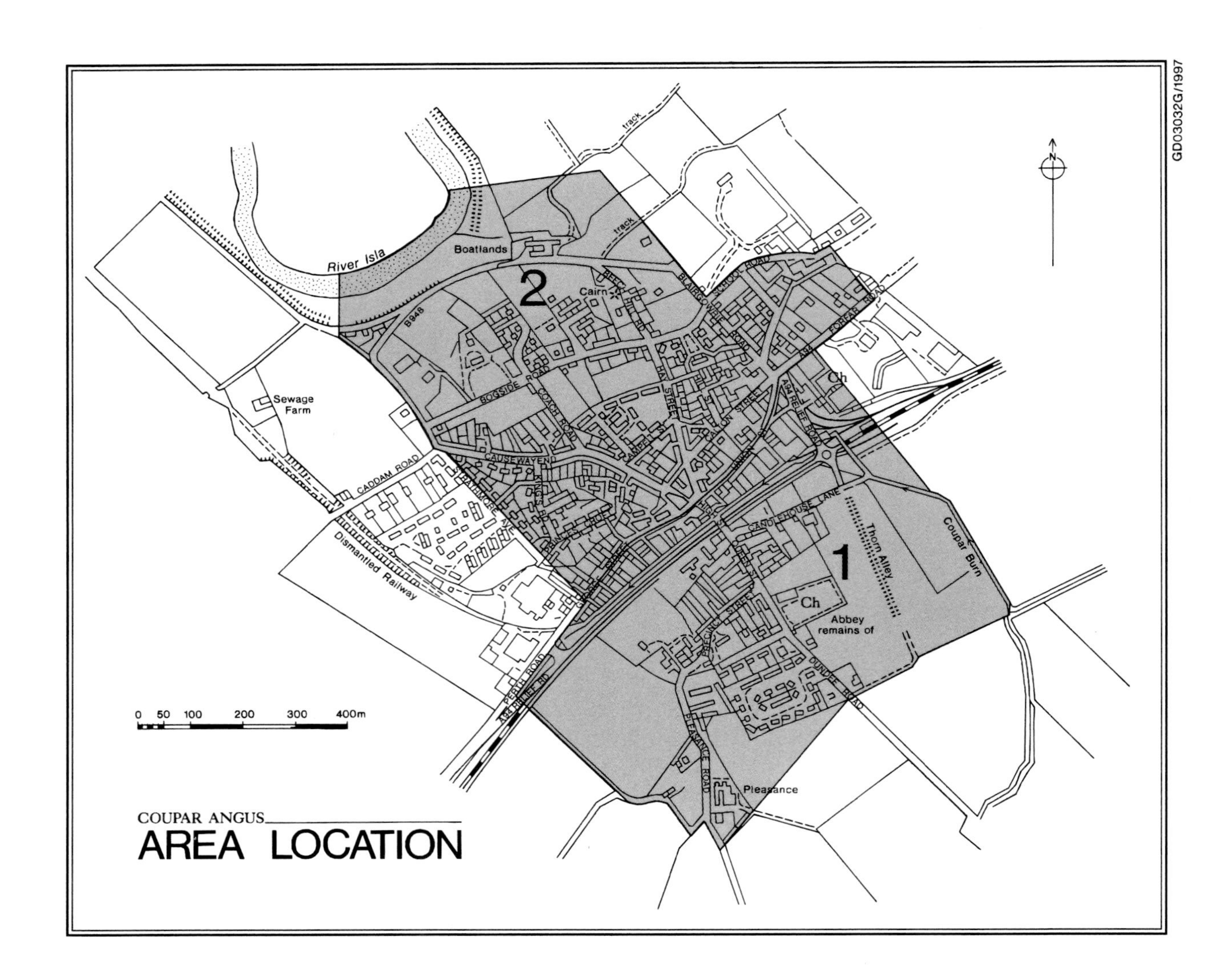

figure 16
Area location map

introduction

The medieval core of the town has been divided up into two areas **figure 16**, with George Street/Union Street as the division. Area 1 lies to the south and Area 2 to the north.

Natural features, such as the Coupar Burn to the south-west and the River Isla to the north, form convenient internal boundaries for the areas under study, but other sub-divisions are more arbitrary in their definition. As George Street/Union Street forms the central division between Areas 1 and 2, both areas overlap to a certain extent, to take in the frontage on the opposite side of the street. This ensures that important features of the medieval townscape, which were often situated in the middle of the street, are not lost in the division between two areas.

area 1

Perth Road/George Street/Union Street/Station Road/Coupar Burn/Cothall Track/Pleasance/Tweedside **figure 17**

description

The High Street, which extends southwards first as Queen Street and then as Dundee Road, sub-divides this area into two halves. To the east of Queen Street lies the present-day parish church **A** with its associated graveyard to the south and east. Immediately north of the church is an area of rough grass known locally as the 'glebe field' **B**. Between the glebe field and Candlehouse Lane is a row of cottages and small villas that front onto Queen Street, with long gardens extending to the rear. Behind the gardens and to the north-east of the glebe land is a small industrial zone **C**, comprising chemical works, stores and a blacksmith's yard. The Strathmore Hotel **D** *&* **figure 13** is situated on the corner of Candlehouse Lane and High Street. Between Candlehouse Lane (recently upgraded to accommodate increased traffic into the industrial zone) and the A94 relief road (**E**) is a largely overgrown grassy area.

Two cultivated fields lie to the east of the glebe field and the churchyard, extending northwards up to Candlehouse Lane and southwards to Cothall Track. Thorn Alley **F**, a raised, grassy bank, separates the two fields, and at the southern end of Thorn Alley is Cothall Track **G**, a pathway that leads along the edge of the fields **figures 4** *&* **17**.

The western side of High Street/Queen Street is predominantly made up of residential housing, a contrasting blend of large Victorian villas and rows of small cottages. The south and western part of Area 1, either side of Pleasance Road, is under cultivation and there is a modern housing development (Abbey Gardens), accessed from

archaeological potential and future development

Many of the development proposals contained within the most recent Coupar Angus Local Plan (1989) have now been completed. The most significant of these was the proposed A94 relief road **E**. This has now opened and was largely constructed on disused railway land. The route of a second relief road **W**, planned for the fields immediately to the east of the abbey church has not, however, been agreed. This road would also be intended to allow greater access to an enlarged industrial zone **C**, situated to the south of Candlehouse Lane. It is possible that the new relief road would sever the fields east of the abbey church, leaving an area difficult to cultivate. These lands would then become available for further housing.

A large area to the east of Queen Street/Dundee Road, extending north to Candlehouse Lane, east to Thorn Alley and south to Cothall Track has been scheduled as a monument of national importance **figure 26**. Any development here will require Scheduled Monument Consent.

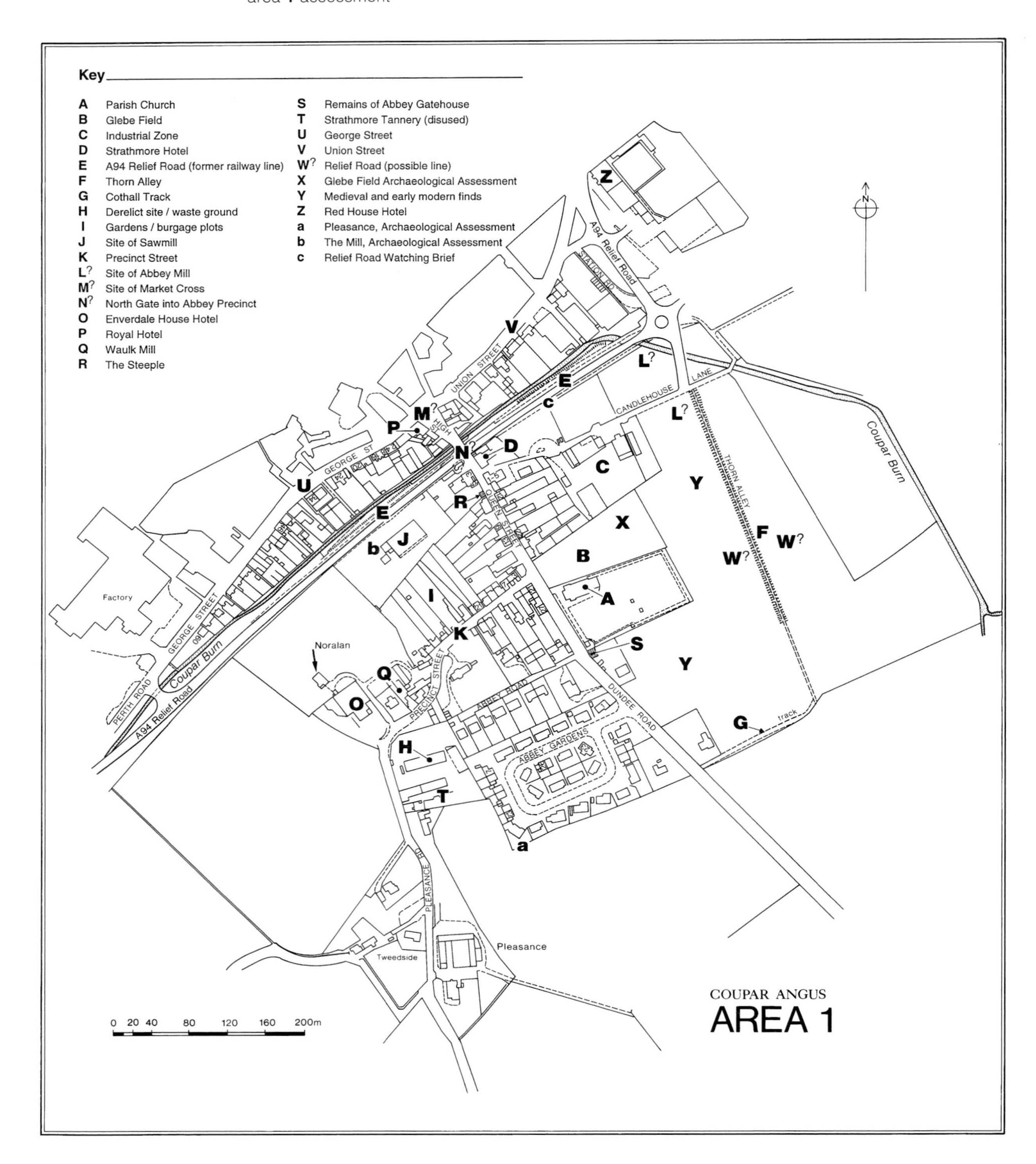

figure 17
Area 1

Dundee Road. North of Abbey Gardens, an unsurfaced road separates a row of modern bungalows on the south side from nineteenth-century cottages and villas on the north side, some set within large gardens that back onto Precinct Street. The south side of Precinct Street comprises small villas, with occasional modern infill. A large area of waste ground **H**, within which lie a number of semi-derelict buildings, is currently in use as a haulage yard. To the south is the now-disused Strathmore Tannery **T**.

history

archaeology

Most of Area 1 is likely to have been contained within the precinct of the abbey and so the archaeological potential is very high. The exact boundaries of the precinct, and of the buildings ranged within it, are still unclear, but modern property boundaries may give some clues as to its possible extent **figures 4 & 17**. Thorn Alley **F**, a long, linear grassy bank to the east of the abbey church, has received much attention as the possible eastern wall

On the north side of Precinct Street **K**, is a row of small cottages extending from the junction of Queen Street to the curve in Precinct Street as it turns southwards. At the western end, some have been converted into small industrial workshops. The gardens of these cottages **I** extend northwards to the edge of a newly constructed residential housing scheme, on the site of the former saw-mill **J**. The A94 relief road forms the northern boundary for this new development, the western boundary being delineated by the extensive fields surrounding the house 'Noralan'.

The remaining part of Area 1 comprises a narrow strip on the north side of the Coupar Burn. This contains the tenement shops and houses that front onto George Street, The Cross and Union Street, with some small plots extending south to the Coupar Burn.

historical background

There was a royal manor at Coupar Angus by at least the reign of David I (1124–53). In 1159, when Malcolm IV allocated territory for the foundation of a Cistercian monastery at Coupar Angus, he set aside 'the royal manor of Coupar in Gowrie'. The existence of a royal grange in this vicinity would, at the very least, suggest the presence of a group of agricultural workers and, perhaps, even an agrarian community.

There may also have been a parish church in the locality. When the Cistercians arrived at Coupar Angus, the bishop of St Andrews surrendered all his rights to this church, in favour of the new abbey. The 'foundation charter' of the abbey, dating to 1161 or 1162, suggests that the church was the kirk of Coupar Angus; but whether it was in Coupar Angus itself or possibly in Bendochy is unclear. A parish church, and one which the bishop of St Andrews considered worthy of a special gesture, would imply the existence of some nearby parishioners.

It seems quite probable that some form of settlement pre-dated the monastery. Once established, the Cistercian complex would have attracted further settlers, who came partly to benefit from the protective aura of the monastic complex but also to fulfil the demand for supplies and commodities a monastic establishment, even one that was largely self-sufficient, created. Lay brothers would have formed an essential part of the monastery, and local people would also have been needed as a workforce. The establishment of a Cistercian monastery in Coupar had a profound effect on the settlement pattern of the area.

Malcolm IV's principal charter, granting his whole land of Coupar, with all its appurtenances, to the Cistercians may be dated to 1161 or 1162. By 1164, a full convent of at least twelve monks arrived from Melrose and an abbot, Fulk, was appointed.

Sometime between 1173 and 1178, William I bestowed a further grant of land: half a ploughgate of land 'ad situm abbacie sue faciendum', which suggests that the abbey was to be built on land not already in the possession of the Cistercians. This would mean that the royal manor of Coupar did not contain the intended site of the abbey. There are two potential implications. The grant may have been merely extending the area of land already given by Malcolm IV; or a gift of land in an area quite separate from the manor of Coupar Angus was now being made. If the latter is the case, it has to be presumed that the Cistercian monks from Melrose settled firstly on the royal manor and later moved to the area now known as Coupar. The manor and the abbey site may not have been far distant; but the possibility exists that they were distinct and separate places.

history

It seems that the monks were not long in establishing themselves. In 1186, rebels against the king were pursued by the earl of Atholl into the abbey of Coupar Angus and

archaeology

of the precinct, or even that of an earlier Roman camp. The tradition of a Roman camp here dates back to the eighteenth century, and although no Roman finds have come to light in any of the recent archaeological excavations **X**, **a** *&* **b**, or in the fieldwalking of the fields to the south of the abbey church, it remains an unproven possibility that the abbey was located on the site of an earlier Roman camp.

figure 18
View of Coupar Angus from the south, published 1843

killed there, before the altar, in defiance of sanctuary, and fifty-eight others were burned in the abbot's quarters. This does not necessarily mean that the monastic complex was fully constructed. Such an undertaking could have taken decades; but it may be significant that the confirmation of a charter of 1196x1207, perhaps 1199, made by Thomas, son of Malcolm of Lundie, specified that if he died in Scotland his body was to be buried at Coupar Angus in 'the cloister before the church door'. This also implies that the cloister and church of the monastery were built by this date. It seems clear from documentary evidence (*see* p 19) that construction work was still going on at the turn of the twelfth and thirteenth centuries. The dedication of the church to St Mary in 1233 would suggest the ecclesiastical building was complete, or near completion.

The completed abbey complex would have consisted of the normal conventual buildings: church, cloister, residence for the abbot, sleeping accommodation for the monks, refectory, guest house and sundry offices. It has been suggested that Cistercian houses also needed a range of further buildings, such as stables, brew-houses, bake-houses and metal-working premises. Amongst Coupar's retainers were a baker, brewer and store-

history

archaeology

Another clue to the extent of the monastic precinct is the supposed gatehouse **figure 23** in the south-west corner of the graveyard, the only upstanding remnant of the abbey **S**. Recent excavations **X** in the glebe field, to the north of the church, conclusively proved this area to have been the graveyard of the abbey. The cloisters must then be located to the south of the present church **A**, which is thought to stand on the site of the medieval abbey church. The area between the present church and the gatehouse is limited, suggesting that this gatehouse led into the main complex of buildings, or into an inner precinct, within which the main buildings were ranged: church, cloister, chapter house, refectory, dormitory, for example, all of which would appear to lie under the present graveyard. The outer precinct may then extend east to Thorn Alley **F**, south to Cothall Track **G**, west to include Abbey Gardens, and north to either Candlehouse Lane or, more probably, to Coupar Burn. The layout within monastic precincts in Scotland is little understood, but a range of activities would have been carried out here; gardens and orchards, meadows, stables, tanneries, brewhouses, ovens, smithies and mills are common features of monastic precincts, and evidence for them may survive in the fields to the east

master, which gives some clues to the associated workshops; although the latter, just as the fowler, land-stewards, foresters, bullock-herds and warreners, may have worked outwith the abbey precinct. Archaeological work has indicated that there may have been a wool-house at Fountains in England. It is quite possible that Coupar also had one. As early as the thirteenth century Douai received wool, valued at £35, from the abbey of 'Cupre'. There is, however, little evidence of the precise lay-out of the complex. It is known that there were various gardens within its walls, including a herb garden and orchard. There was, as well, a dovecot yard and a mustard yard, and probably other gardens. There was also an outer yard to the abbey, set at the west side of the complex, and a porter's lodge. All the indications suggest an extensive establishment and the present 'Precinct Street' **K** may well reflect an earlier occupation by the monastery, indicating that the monastic lands spread well to the west. The exact dimensions of the abbey complex, however, are unknown, although it would be expected that the Coupar Burn was within the area of the precinct, as this would be an ideal supply of water for general purposes, as well as for running the abbey's mill **L**.

The abbey was a wealthy establishment and on a number of occasions played host to royalty (*see* p 19). It also had an impact on more ordinary people. As an important landowner, which exported its produce overseas and had an agricultural surplus, its function as the focus of a market held implications for the surrounding hinterland. How soon a market was established at its gate is unclear. By 1352, however, the fair at Coupar Abbey was proving detrimental to Dundee's trade; and in 1359 David II issued a charter to Dundee prohibiting Coupar Angus, Kettins, Kirriemuir and Alyth to hold markets since they were within the liberty of Dundee, which had the sole right to sell wool and skins and deal with foreign merchants within the sheriffdom of Forfar. It seems that such measures were largely ignored: the market continued, the bishop of Dunkeld, for example, buying boards for a church roof there in 1506. Fruit trees were also purchased for the king's residence at Stirling, but whether at the market or not is unclear.

Coupar's market was held 'at the gate of the monastery every Friday'. The red cross stood to the north of the abbey precincts. An important landmark, it was probably also the market cross **M**. It certainly functioned as the focal point of settlement. A regular market would have attracted not only traders but also craftsmen to settle in its vicinity; and it can be safely assumed that this factor, as well as the presence of the abbey, encouraged the growth of a lay settlement at the abbey's north gate **N**.

There are some indications that, from the fourteenth century, the monastery did not continue to prosper as it had initially. But repair and maintenance work continued, although somewhat spasmodically (*see* p22).

It is unclear whether there was an attack on the monastic buildings at the time of the Reformation. In 1563, a catalogue of repairs was recorded. These included repairing the

history

archaeology

of the present church or to the west of the main road which now splits the precinct in two. Access to water was vital, so it seems likely that the precinct would have extended up to and included the Coupar Burn. Water drawn from the burn would also provide power for the mills, and a complex network of drains and lades would have traversed the precinct.

Monitoring of further development within the precinct is essential if the inner workings of this monastic settlement are to be understood. Remains of the precinct boundary, out-buildings and other features here are likely to be preserved, not only in the fields and open areas (like the glebe field), but also beneath the houses that have gradually infilled the precinct since the Reformation. The streets are a later addition and features may also be preserved here, sealed beneath the modern road surface. The new relief road **E**, a significant new addition to the town plan, did not, however, disturb archaeological deposits to any great extent **C** as it largely followed the line of the disused railway. The most archaeologically sensitive area is around the present parish church and graveyard, which appear to have been built over the main complex of abbey buildings. Development in the church and graveyard is unlikely, but the need for environmental improvements, such as new services, is likely and must be closely monitored.

granaries and stables (which may not have been situated at the abbey grange), the stacking of slates in the cloister, blocking of doorways to prevent access to looters of timber from the church and steeple, and renewing the abbot's windows. However, there could not have been wholesale devastation as the abbey had been a suitable abode for Queen Mary in 1562.

How much these events at, and after, the Reformation affected the people in the township of Coupar Angus is unclear. It has been suggested that the abbey church had already begun to function as the church for the local folk; and they may also have been using the abbey graveyard as their burial ground **B**. Possible children's graves found during recent excavations might support this theory (*see* p 23). The portioning out of abbey estates at a distance from the township probably had little impact on the lives of the local people; the dividing up of monastic lands in the township itself was more likely to have an effect. In 1573, for example, sasine was given on the outer yard of the monastery, which stood to the west of the outer gate, outwith the walls of the monastery.

There is clear indication that the market continued to function after the Reformation (*see* p 24). The old market cross still maintained its significant role, not only as the focal point for the market, but also as the place where important declarations of public interest were made. With the attaining of burgh status in 1607 (*see* pp 23–4) the burgesses of Coupar Angus were to have the right to trade freely, with markets and four three-day fairs. There was to be a tolbooth and a market cross, the secular focal points of the burgh.

The market appears to have continued to function without hiatus. The customs or tolls were clearly imposed regularly; and a reference to the customs of Coupar's markets (plural) suggests an element of specialisation. a 'trein mercat' or timber market is known to have existed in Coupar from at least the sixteenth century and was still functioning in 1605. On 28 November 1616, John Forrester, bailie, held the court of the 'land and lordship of Coupar'. It was laid down that any fleshers that brought decaying meat to the market at Coupar would be brought to court and fined £5, which might imply a specific meat market; although the fleshers could merely have been attending the general market, which was held weekly, on Fridays at this time.

The tolbooth was the building where dues, or tolls, to use the market were collected.

history

How soon Lord Coupar, the burgh superior, erected it is uncertain. There is a reference in

archaeology

It is also important to trace how settlement developed here in the post-Reformation period. Evidence for this may also be contained both beneath and within the fabric of existing standing buildings, for example along High Street and Precinct Street. Here, earlier floor levels may be preserved below present floors, and perhaps earlier buildings too.

The modern street pattern, where a number of streets converge at The Cross, and where the market cross **M** may also have stood, appears to indicate the approximate position of the main gateway into the abbey precinct **N**. The remains of this structure, since robbed for its stone, and indeed the precinct wall itself, may survive sealed below the modern street level.

Medieval settlement in Coupar Angus, contemporary with the abbey, is likely to have centred around The Cross. The street frontages of George Street and Union Street are, therefore, particularly sensitive to further development and must be monitored. The remains of this early settlement, where the craftsmen and their families who provided services to the abbey lived, may be preserved beneath the floors and within the fabric of existing standing buildings.

In other towns, recent excavations have revealed street frontages as the most promising for preservation of archaeological deposits, in spite of the problem of cellarage which may have destroyed evidence. Although there has been no opportunity to examine any of the street frontages in Coupar Angus, evidence of medieval structures in the form of post-holes and floor surfaces may be expected, sealed beneath eighteenth- or nineteenth-century standing buildings such as The Royal Hotel **P figure 12**, Strathmore Hotel **D figure**

the *Records of the Privy Council* in 1619 to the tolbooth, market cross and stocks of Coupar; but, although indexed as 'Coupar Angus', the text refers merely to 'Couper' and there may here be a confusion with Cupar in Fife. Two years later, however, in the same source there is mention of Lord Ogilvie of Airlie, bailie principal of the Lordship of Coupar, and his deputies holding courts in the tolbooth of the burgh. Precisely where it was sited is unknown, but it can be reasonably expected that it was near to the market cross.

Documentary evidence also indicates that Coupar's corn mill, on Coupar Burn, established long previously by the abbey, continued to function.

Lord Coupar appears to have maintained his household on abbey property and possibly the abbot's quarters would have been the most suitable. This is also further evidence that the supposed destruction at the Reformation has been highly exaggerated (*see* p 22). The Protestant minister lived in the town, in a dwelling house with a yard. Its location is not known.

In 1618, James VI confirmed the lordship of Coupar. At the special request of the king, Lord Coupar agreed that, as the parish of Bendochy was divided by the Water of Isla and as it was sometimes dangerous for those parishioners south of the river to attend the parish church at Bendochy, he would build a new kirk within the precincts of the monastery, to be called the kirk of Coupar, to serve as the parish church for Coupar and the parish of Bendochy south of the Isla. He also agreed to provide the minister with a manse and a glebe and a stipend of 500 merks; in return he would have the hereditary right of patronage to the new parish church. The fact that he agreed to build a new church suggests that the abbey church was, by this time, beyond repair.

Lord Coupar was a supporter of the Covenanters; and, in April 1645, 200 men, led by Sir Alexander Macdonald and Forbes of Skellater, descended on Coupar Angus, with the intention of teaching Lord Coupar a lesson. He was not at home, but the minister and others were killed; the town was 'fyrit'; and the residence of Lord Coupar was attacked. How great an effect this had on the material fabric of the town is not documented. As the town was burnt, many buildings would have had to be repaired or even replaced. The abbey structures, whether in ruins or still partially standing, may have been useful quarries. Many of the town's domestic buildings, to this day, reveal that they were partially or entirely built of erstwhile abbey stone.

13 and The Steeple **R figure 14** (*see* pp 59–61). Recent excavations in Perth, Dunfermline and Arbroath have also shown that the width and alignment of the main streets in burghs have changed over the centuries. Earlier cobbled street surfaces and contemporary buildings may, therefore, be preserved up to three or four metres behind the line of the modern street frontage.

Within these and other standing buildings in the medieval core of the town, the remains of floor surfaces and other features associated with earlier phases of occupation may be preserved, sealed beneath the modern floor levels. Features may also be sealed within the fabric itself, blocked off by later additions. The foundations of earlier buildings which pre-date the present standing buildings may also survive, buried beneath present floor levels.

Burgage plots are often a valuable source of information, yielding evidence about everyday life in the medieval period. The contents of rubbish pits and middens, common features of burgage plots, can provide details of diet and living conditions, for example. Traces of these plots, which slope gently down to the Coupar Burn, may survive behind the south of the George Street/Union Street frontage. Later in date, but important for our understanding of both the abbey precinct and post-Reformation settlement here, are the burgage plots that extend north from the Precinct Street frontage **I**. These appear to have survived largely intact and any development should be monitored closely.

Finally, the discovery of a Bronze Age cist in the graveyard of the parish church **A**, together with other chance finds such as a flint scraper and whetstone, indicates the continuing potential for prehistoric remains in this area.

The available evidence seems to suggest that Lord Coupar permitted his residence to fall into disrepair after the 1645 attack. How much damage was done is not clear, although it is known that it was 'spoiled and plundered'. His nephew, John, third Lord Balmerino, who succeeded him in 1669, felt it necessary to charge Lord Coupar's widow 'to repair and put in order the manor place of Coupar'. Little seems to have been achieved; and in the mid 1680s it was described as having been 'a very sweet place ... in very pleasant countryside' but 'now nothing but rubbish'.

It seems that Lord Coupar did not fulfil his promise to erect a new parish church for the residents south of the Isla. In 1683, the bishop of Dunkeld set up a commission of ministers, wrights and masons to inspect the kirk of Coupar. They declared that it was 'quite ruinous' and 'altogether unsafe to come to hear sermon in it'. They estimated that it would cost six times as much to repair as it would to put up a new building in the churchyard. From April 1683, because of the state of the kirk's fabric, services were to be held in 'the low vaults of the abbay'. During that year a number of improvements were effected to this 'laigh abbey': a pulpit and reader's seat were moved in; doors were added and some masonry work done; glass was put in the window at the gable where the pulpit stood and another little window was glazed. Although it is clear that some repair work had to be done to make the vault adequately comfortable for worship, the state of the 'laigh abbey' was, at least, relatively wind and water-tight, which suggests, yet again, that Reformation damage has been exaggerated. In 1685, Mr George Hay, minister, complained to Lord Balmerino that Lord Coupar had, instead of building, merely allotted one of his own 'ruinous office-houses which was above the gate' and that it 'was

previous archaeological work and chance finds

The following entries have been extracted from the Royal Commission database (RCAHMS, National Monuments Record of Scotland). The Commission's record card numbering system has also been included (in brackets) for further reference.

prehistoric finds in the vicinity of Coupar Angus Abbey, NO *224 398*

cist
A cist *c* 2.1 m long by *c* 0.6 m broad was discovered in 1887, about 1.8 m below ground level, within the burial-ground at Coupar Angus Abbey, but beyond the limits of the abbey walls. It had no cover, but was paved, while the sides were made up of blue stone slabs, set on edge. Hutcheson (1888), 147.

whetstone
A small Bronze Age whetstone of quartzite was found in the burial ground of Coupar Angus Abbey, at a depth of *c* 1.8 m, several yards to the south of a long cist found earlier that year, 1887. It was broken at the butt end and measured *c* 7 cm in length when purchased for the National Museums of Scotland. Hutcheson (1888), 147.

Coupar Angus Abbey, NO *223 397*

abbey
All that remains of the abbey is a fragment of a supposed gatehouse **S** *&* **figure 23**.

Within and around the standing 1859/60 parish church there are a number of architectural fragments of thirteenth- to sixteenth-century date and several carved stones, notably the grave-slab of Abbot John Schanwel (d 1506), the effigy of Sir Thomas Hay of Errol, a man-at-arms, two figures in civilian dress and a sixth figure bearing an axe.

In the late eighteenth century 'digging at the west end of the church' revealed over twelve stone coffins, whilst in 1887 two more stone coffins and a possible long cist were found in the burial ground. (NMRS NO 23 NW 13).

dangerous to be in'. The heritors were instructed to build a new one, 'in the abbey cemetery'; and also a school house, above the former prison.

Most of the heritors appeared willing to oblige and stented themselves at £28 per £100 of valued rent. This was a high rate, which bore rewards. Three masons started work in May 1686. They were to commence with digging the foundations, with the help of two barrowmen; another man was to demolish the walls of the old church; the stones were to be carried to the new site; and another local man was to dig and carry the mortar. By the following December, the minister reported that since 'the fabrick and rooff' of the new church were now complete, worship would commence. The following Sunday, the bishop of Aberdeen preached in the new kirk **A**.

Some carvings from the original abbey church were moved into the new building; and in spite of post seventeenth-century rebuilding of the church (*see* p29 & 30) these may still be viewed. The tomb slab of Abbot John Schanwel, who died in 1506, and the effigy of Sir Thomas Hay of Errol, third Hay constable of Scotland survive.

Records of this time indicate clearly that, with the destruction of much of the abbey complex, there had been colonisation in the abbey precincts. A small suburb called 'The Precinct' had grown up, probably near to the present Precinct Street **K**.

Some standing buildings are still reminders of Coupar's past (*see* pp 59–63). The Royal Hotel **P** & **figure 12**, originally called the Defiance Inn, took its first name from the stage-coach which stopped here daily on the Edinburgh–Perth–Aberdeen run. Across the road, the White House or White Horse Inn, now the Strathmore Hotel **D** & **figure 13**, was also a hostelry for travellers. A few remnants of the stables and tethering rings are still visible at

history

archaeology

Thorn Alley, enclosure **F**

Situated around 80 m ENE of the burial ground adjoining the nineteenth-century parish church **A**, and extending a distance of 280 m from NNW to SSE, there are the turf-covered remains of what may have been a substantial stone wall. It is the surviving portion of what was thought by antiquarians to be a Roman military earthwork, and described by Maitland in 1757 as 'an equilateral quadrangle'. The OSA describes it as a nearly regular square of 24 acres.

The earthwork may have been a monastic enclosure around the Cistercian Abbey, but it is also possible that it originated as a Roman temporary camp. *RCAHMS* (1994), 86, 128, 160.

abbey boundary, Pleasance, Coupar Angus NO 224 396 **a**

In advance of building operations, a section was cut through the supposed southern boundary of the abbey precinct, 60 m west of the Dundee–Coupar Angus road (A293). The objectives were to investigate its construction and the possible existence within the same boundaries of a Roman marching camp. A flat-bottomed, U-shaped ditch 2.1 m deep was revealed, containing nineteenth-century pottery. *DES* (1974), 53.

medieval and early modern coins NO 224 397 **Y**

Six coins and one jeton were found in the field to the east of the site of Coupar Angus Abbey.

(i) William the Lion silver penny of late twelfth/early thirteenth century, moneyer Hue Walter, mint possibly Roxburgh. (ii) Henry III silver cut halfpenny, Short Cross, Class 7, *c* 1218–42. (iii) James III copper black farthing, first issue 1465–6. (iv) James II/III copper 'ecclesiastical farthing', second half of the fifteenth century. (v) Copper alloy Nuremberg jeton, probably late fifteenth century. (vi) Louis XIII copper double *tournois* of 1611. (vii) Charles I copper turner, first issue, 1629. All the coins were returned to their finders. *DES* (1992), 76.

history

the rear. The Steeple **R** & **figure 14**, or tolbooth tower, was built by public subscription in 1762 and completed in 1769. It is purportedly on the site of the former High Court of Justiciary, and was built to serve as a gaol on the ground floor and as a meeting house for local courts on the upper floors. Although later falling into partial ruin, much of the original of the Steeple remains.

The parish also considered itself to have sufficient resources to substantially rebuild the church in the 1780s. It was at this time that one of the remaining parts of the old abbey was removed—'an arch, of beautiful architecture, situate near the centre of the ... churchyard, was demolished for the purpose of furnishing stones for the ... church'. A visitor in the 1790s noted vestiges of the abbey still standing, but whether there was substantially more than remains today is unclear **S** & **figure 18**. Sometime in the 1820s, the watch-tower in the kirkyard was built to shelter watchmen on the look-out for grave-robbers.

Coupar's contacts with the rest of Scotland were much easier after the opening of the railway **E** in 1837. The Newtyle and Coupar Angus Railway Company had been incorporated in 1835, employing the local surveyor, William Blackadder. Although its seal depicts a locomotive surrounded with the symbols of speed and time and carries the motto, 'Time is Precious', the service was horse-drawn for much of the time until it was incorporated in 1847 into the Dundee, Perth and Aberdeen Railway Junction Company. The railway was to have an impact not only on the life of the Coupar people, but also on

archaeology

medieval and early modern finds NO 224 397 **Y**

A number of medieval finds have been made on Meadowside Farm in the field to the east of the site of Coupar Angus Abbey. These include white gritty pottery, oyster shells, a butchered cattle tibia, a decorative bronze mount, a trefoil-shaped horse-harness pendant, an enamelled copper alloy mount in the shape of a shield, a copper alloy strap end and a small copper alloy bell. Also found were a heart-shaped copper alloy mount with the incised letters 'dc', probably of sixteenth- or seventeenth-century date, and a William and Mary turner of 1691–4. A late fifteenth- or early sixteenth-century lead seal matrix from this site has been allocated to Perth Museum and Art Gallery as treasure trove. All other material has been donated to Perth Museum and Art Gallery. *DES* (1992), 76.

Fieldwalking in 1993, organised by the Council for Scottish Archaeology and Perth Museum and Art Gallery on the supposed southern range of Coupar Angus Abbey to the south of the present church and graveyard, led to a number of medieval finds. These included medieval pottery, slag, mortar, stone roof tiles (some with peg holes) and midden material, including oyster shells, a scallop shell and animal bone. A prehistoric flint scraper was also among the finds. Finds and archive held by Perth Museum and Art Gallery. *DES* (1993), 100.

The glebe field NO 223 398 **B**, **X**

cemetery and buried landscape features
An archaeological assessment of the glebe field, funded by Historic Scotland, was carried out in advance of a proposed housing development by East Perthshire Housing Association. The field, approximately 0.7 ha in area, lies to the north of the present nineteenth-century parish church but within the precinct of the medieval abbey. The principal discovery was a cemetery containing an estimated 400–600 burials. Exactly when the bodies were interred is uncertain and, other than a few sherds of medieval

the townscape. The line cut straight across the top of the High Street, where level crossing gates operated **figure 14**. To serve the needs of passengers, the Railway Hotel was built with six rooms to let, a dining room and a bar. Now much extended and altered, it is called the Red House Hotel **Z**.

Many other changes were to be made to the townscape. New access roads, George Street **U** to the west leading to Perth and Union Street **V** to the east of The Cross relieved some of the congestion in the old main thoroughfare, Calton Street.

Still standing are buildings which give a feel of nineteenth-century Coupar Angus (*see* pp 61–3). The eighteenth-century restored church was replaced by the present Victorian church in 1859, built to the design of local architect John Carver. Private dwelling houses at The Cross, in George Street and in Union Street also stand testament to the domestic building quality of the town (*see* pp 61–3). By the late nineteenth century, the town had three linen works, a tannery **T**, farina works and sawmills **J**. There was also a waulk mill **Q** north of Precinct Street, fed by a lade from Coupar Burn in the south-east, the water being controlled by sluice gates. The water left the mill in an open lade and then flowed back into the burn, to the north. One of the manufactories, the Strathmore Linen Works, was a quality building, demolished as recently as 1984. The home of the owners, the McFarlanes, built in 1875, still stands, although much altered and extended as Enverdale House Hotel **O**.

history

archaeology

pottery, few dateable finds were recovered. The cemetery was, however, found to have been established over landfill dumps, probably associated with the building of the abbey, and a series of ditched features cut through a buried medieval land surface. In all, forty-eight burials were recorded in a small sample of the total development area. The status of the cemetery remains uncertain, as the burials seem to include children and juveniles. It may be associated with the abbey. Alternatively, it may be a late medieval or early modern lay cemetery serving the townspeople of Coupar Angus. O'Sullivan (1995), 1045–1068.

The Mill, Queen Street NO 221 398 **b**

An archaeological assessment was carried out on this site in 1994, which may have lain within the northern sector of the abbey precinct. Unfortunately, the site had been heavily truncated when in use as a sawmill **J** and few features of archaeological interest were recorded. The most significant was a shallow, north to south aligned ditch, the fill of which contained a sherd of green-glazed medieval pottery. Rees & Duffy (1994), 27.

Candlehouse Lane NO 223 399 **c**

post-medieval drain

In compliance with Scheduled Monument Consent, a watching brief was carried out on construction works for the new Coupar Angus relief road (A94). The line of the new road re-used the former railway track but passed close by the northern edge of the Coupar Angus Abbey scheduled area and the supposed north boundary of the abbey precinct. A stone-lined drain, probably nineteenth century in date, was found during the cutting of a section of the road adjacent to the north of Candlehouse Lane. Pottery from the drain fills indicated a nineteenth-century date for the drain. No medieval features or finds were identified during the watching brief. *DES* (1996), 83.

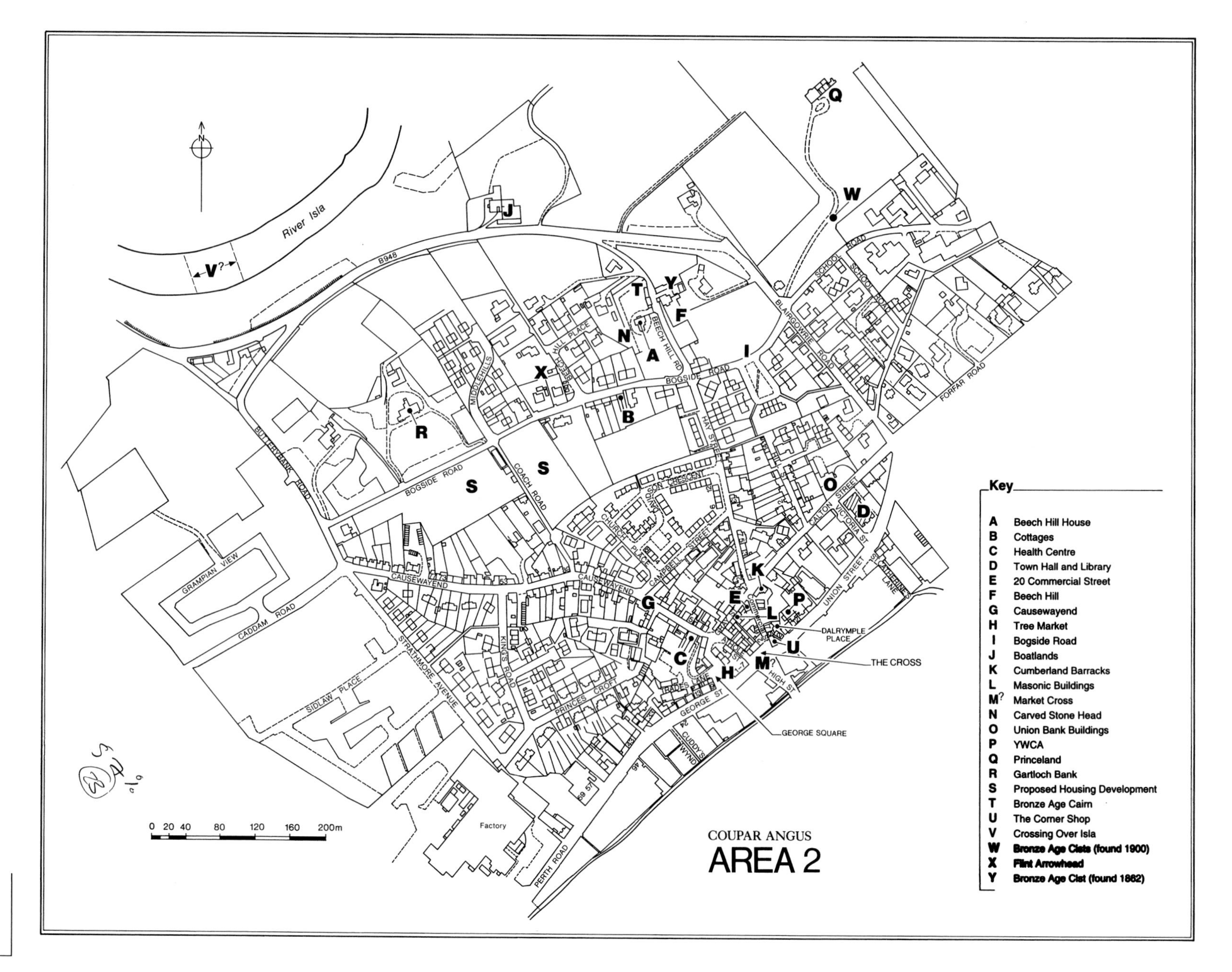

figure 19
Area 2

area 2

George Street/Union Street/Forfar Road/School Road/Blairgowrie Road/River Isla (north bank)/ Strathmore Avenue **figure 19**

description

This is the main commercial and residential area of the town, which has seen some new development in recent years. The conservation area incorporates The Cross, George Square, Gray Street, Union Street, Calton Street, Commercial Street and Hay Street.

At the northern end of this area, north of Bogside Road, the ground rises up to a long ridge that runs approximately east to west. Beech Hill House **figure 19.A** stands on this ridge overlooking both the town to the south and the River Isla to the north. More rural than urban, this part of the town was popular in the Victorian period, attracting a number of substantial villas. The area between Middlehills and Beech Hill Road, however, has since been infilled with a modern housing development.

The south side of Bogside Road is largely undeveloped, with the exception of one row of small cottages opposite Beech Hill Place **B**. A modern housing development now occupies the area between Church Place and Hay Street, and also on the corner of Hay Street and Bogside Road.

Causewayend retains much of its character, with rows of small cottages lining the narrow, winding street. To the south and west, the block comprising Strathmore Avenue, Causewayend and Princes Croft is now largely modern housing. Trades Lane, which lies behind the George Street frontage (north side), is in a rather dilapidated state, with a number of boarded-up properties. North of Trades Lane is the new health centre **C**, which also fronts onto Causewayend.

At the eastern end of Area 2, to the west of and fronting onto Blairgowrie Road, are a number of large Victorian villas. Similarly, large villas front onto both Union Street and Calton Street. The Town Hall and library **D** & **figure 20** are situated on the corner of Union Street and Victoria Street.

The remaining part of Area 2 is centred around The Cross. Here, the narrow streets and 'islands' of buildings add character to the town but make access for traffic extremely difficult. Some of the buildings have been restored and red sandstone, robbed from the abbey after the Reformation, can clearly be seen.

historical background

For a detailed account of the background history of Coupar Angus and its abbey, *see* pp 17–26.

The red cross stood to the north of the abbey precincts. This presumed site of the market cross **M** marked an important landmark; it was used as the point from which the barony of Keithick was divided, thus placing Coupar Angus, or Baitscheill (Beech Hill), at the centre of the barony, and it functioned as the focal point of settlement.

Baitscheill appears frequently in the abbey's records from the fifteenth century onwards; it may perhaps have designated the whole area to the north of the abbey as far as the Isla.

archaeological potential and future development

The Coupar Angus Local Plan (1989) includes only one development proposal for this area. The south side of Bogside Road, comprising two large fields has been identified as suitable for local authority housing, sheltered housing or housing association development **S**.

No archaeological work has been undertaken in this area other than the excavation of the cairn **T** at Beech Hill House **figures 5 & 6**. As a result, the archaeological potential of the medieval core of Coupar Angus, probably concentrated around The Cross, is extremely difficult to assess.

figure 20
Town Hall, Queen Street, in the early twentieth century

history

Coupar's market was held 'at the gate of the monastery every Friday'. A regular market would have attracted not only traders, but also craftsmen, to settle in its vicinity. It can be safely assumed that this factor, as well as the presence of the abbey, encouraged the growth of a lay settlement at the abbey's north gate. It would not have been unique for a small township to grow up beside a Scottish Cistercian house; Culross and Kinloss both emerged beside a Cistercian nucleus. According to local tradition, the Coupar people, at this time, were subject to the authority of the abbot through his regality court, said to have met on the mound at Beech Hill (Baitscheill) **F**. The market continued to function after the Reformation. The old market cross still maintained its significant role, not only as the focal point for the market, but also as the place where important declarations of public interest were made.

A charter of 1581 refers to 'the tenants of Baitscheill [Beech Hill] and Calsayend [Causewayend]' **G**. Clearly, there were already established two closely related settlements at Coupar, even if these suburbs would not have been intensively developed. When John Porter had been appointed as hereditary porter to the abbey, sometime between 1480 and 1509, he had been granted, amongst other things, a dwelling house at Baitscheill with six acres of arable land and pasturage for two horses and seven cows and their young, which suggests a particularly rural atmosphere. Primary source material indicates, also, that close by Calsayend (Causewayend) the 'treyn-mercat' (tree market) had already been established by the sixteenth century **H**.

In 1607, the temporal lordship of James Elphinstone, second son of the first Lord Balmerino, created for him out of the remaining lands and baronies of the abbey (*see* pp 23 *&* 24), was constituted a burgh of barony. Elphinstone received the title of Baron Coupar. With burghal status, Lord Coupar was to have the right to appoint bailies, a treasurer and a dean of guild, as well as 'consules', which may be interpreted either as bailies or as members of a burgh council. Burgesses were to be made; and they were to have the right to trade freely, with markets and four three-day fairs. There was to be a tolbooth and a market cross, the secular focal points of the burgh. The new burgh

archaeology

In other towns, recent excavations have revealed street frontages as the most promising for preservation of archaeological deposits, in spite of the problem of cellarage which can destroy earlier evidence. Although there has been no opportunity to examine any of the street frontages in Coupar Angus, evidence of medieval structures in the form of post-holes and floor surfaces may be expected, sealed beneath the eighteenth- or nineteenth-century standing buildings such as 'The Corner Shop' **U** on The Cross, *no* 20 Commercial Street **E** and the Masonic Buildings in Gray Street **L**. Recent excavations in Perth, Dunfermline and Arbroath have also shown that the width and alignment of the main streets in burghs have changed over the centuries. Earlier cobbled street surfaces and contemporary buildings may therefore be preserved up to three or four metres behind the line of the modern street frontage.

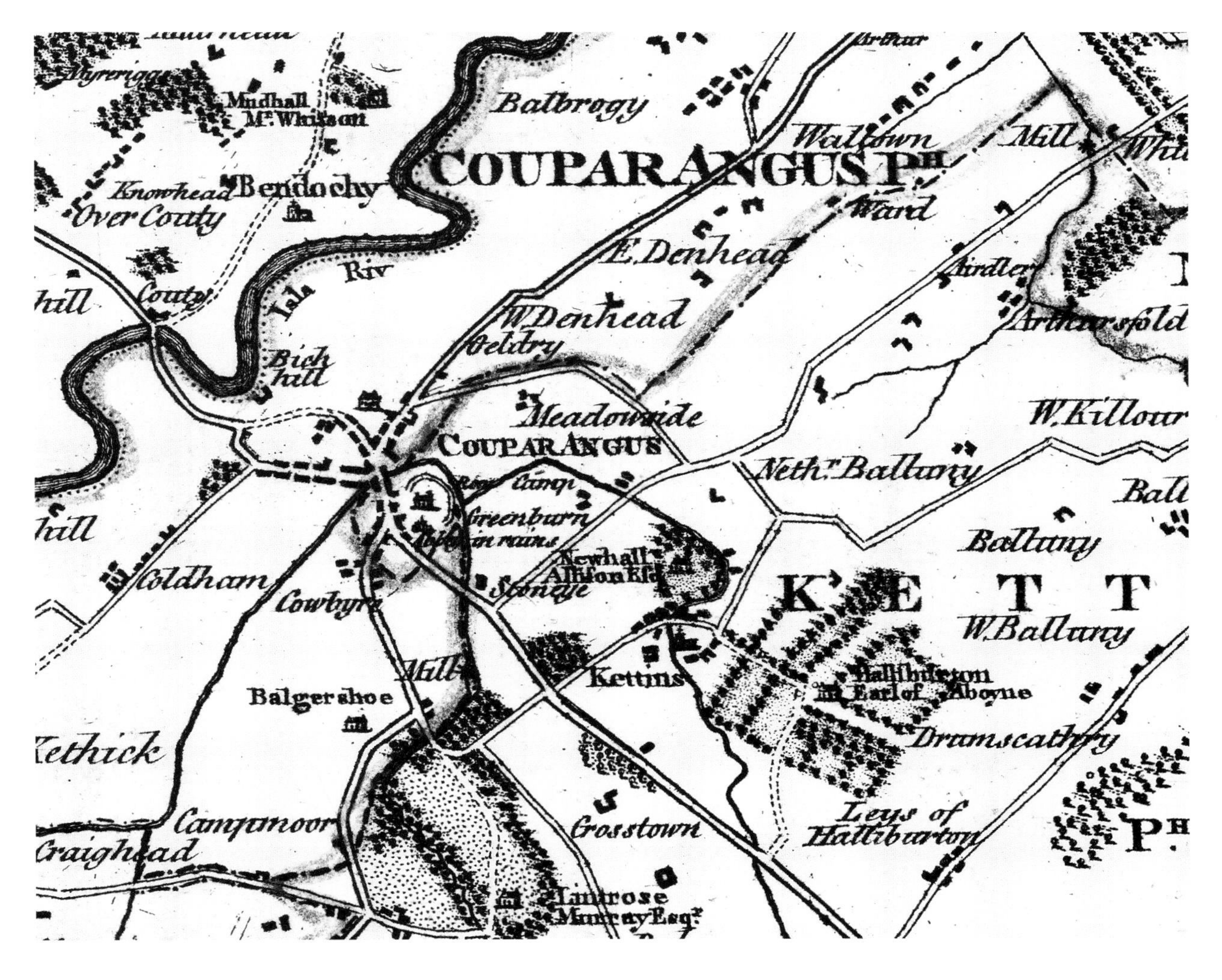

figure 21
Detail from J Ainslie's map of the county of Forfar 1794

history

superior was also to have the right to grant out burgh lands, hold courts and dispense justice and punishments in his burgh.

Lack of burgh records for this period leave it unclear whether there was, at this point, a formal allocation of lands—burgage plots or tofts—to the new burgesses, who might have been incomers as well as natives of Coupar Angus. It would have been in Lord Coupar's interest to encourage a strong, economically viable sub- structure to his new burgh and this could have been attained by the offer of burghal privileges and property. This makes it likely that the population rose during the first decades of the seventeenth century. Incomers would have required land on which to build their dwellings; and probably these plots or tofts were measured out by burghal officers called liners.

It is known that a market cross already existed; its position within the town setting and Coupar's street pattern is interesting. Unlike the majority of Scottish medieval and early-modern towns, which had an axial main street with back lanes running parallel and burgage plots set in herring-bone pattern from the main street, Coupar's streets radiate out from a central point, The Cross **figures 19 & 21**. This probably evolved at the

archaeology

Within these and other standing buildings in the medieval core of the town, the remains of floor surfaces and other features associated with earlier phases of occupation may be preserved, sealed beneath the modern floor levels. Features may also be sealed within the fabric itself, blocked off by latter additions. The Cumberland Barracks **K & figure 11** has seen two phases of construction in its history, and features from the earliest phase may be concealed behind later alterations. The foundations of earlier buildings which pre-date the present standing buildings may also survive, buried beneath present floor levels.

The most archaeologically sensitive areas are likely to be concentrated around The Cross and George Square. Settlement would also have clustered along the main routes into town, notably Causewayend, as this may have been the main road from the crossing intersection of important thoroughfares—from Perth, Dundee and from the north via the ferry-boat crossing or the fording point across the Isla. Until recent years, the flood stone that indicated water level at the ford was visible. To this day, in the dry season, the causey stones of the ford are clearly to be seen, a little to the east of Bendochy church. It was probably via this route that the abbots had passed to one of their two country seats—Coupar Grange. The route to Dundee, on the other hand, could not originally have been aligned as at present, as the abbey complex occupied an area that encompassed the present Dundee Road; the current road to Perth, George Street, is a modern development, as is Union Street. Calton Street was the original main east-west thoroughfare. These routeways converged on the focal point of the settlement at the now defunct abbey gates—the market cross.

The market appears to have continued to function without hiatus. The customs or tolls were clearly imposed regularly; and a reference to the customs of Coupar's markets (plural) suggests an element of specialisation. On 28 November 1616, John Forrester, bailie, held the court of the 'land and lordship of Coupar'. It was laid down that any fleshers who brought decaying meat to the market at Coupar would be brought to court and fined £5. This might imply a specific meat market, although the fleshers could merely have been attending the general market, which was held weekly, on Fridays at this time.

The tolbooth was the building where dues, or tolls, to use the market were collected. There is no mention in the records of a medieval tolbooth, but in 1607 Lord Coupar was given the right to erect one (*see* p 24). How soon this was achieved is uncertain. There is a reference in the *Records of the Privy Council* in 1619 to the tolbooth, market cross and stocks of Coupar; but, although indexed as 'Coupar Angus', the text refers merely to 'Couper' and there may be a confusion with Cupar in Fife. Two years later, however, in the same source there is mention of Lord Ogilvie of Airlie, bailie principal of the Lordship of Coupar, and his deputies holding courts in the tolbooth of the burgh. Precisely where the tolbooth stood is unclear, but it is safe to assume that it was somewhere near the market cross.

Although it is not possible to completely recreate a town plan, the little available documentary evidence available suggests that, by the latter half of the seventeenth century, a number of streets led to or stood near the market cross. There were at least three streets to the east of the cross, which may have been cobbled, since they are referred to as 'causeys'. Another street was called 'Market Wynd'. The fact that a tenement of land, named 'the outsteid', on this street had a croft of land to its north is clear indication that there was little congestion in the market centre. To the west of this tenement and

history

archaeology

of the River Isla **V**, although a strong case can be put for a fording point further east of Bendochy parish church (*see* p 24). Early settlement may also have been attracted to Commercial Street/Hay Street, the main route down from Beech Hill, which would have been on a routeway from this latter ford.

Burgage plots are often a valuable source of information, yielding evidence about everyday life in the medieval period. The contents of rubbish pits and middens, common features of burgage plots, can provide detail of diet and living conditions, for example. These plots often become 'fossilised' as back gardens in many historic towns. Unfortunately, few, if any, examples can be seen in this part of Coupar Angus, although some may survive along the northern end of Causewayend.

The most important features of medieval townscapes were situated in the middle of the street: the ports, tolbooth, market place, market cross, tron and wells, for example. The streets and wynds are, therefore, important as an archaeological resource, and are particularly sensitive to environmental improvements (especially as there is, in the case of Coupar Angus, no extant evidence of ports).

The Bronze Age cairn **T** on Beech Hill, and the discovery of cists in the vicinity **W**, indicate the attractiveness of Beech Hill in prehistory. The recent excavation of the cairn **figures 5 & 6** established a long sequence of activity here, spanning the late Neolithic

croft, a routeway called the 'Stripe' led to Causewayend (Calseyend); and the 'Common hie way' to Causewayend lay to its east. This road had houses, a barn, a malt-house and a kiln, at least, on its west frontage. West of the market place was the timber or tree market **H**. This, too, was bounded on its north by tenements and at least one croft. Between the timber market and market place there were tenements and other buildings, including a carpenter's premises and 'shopmanstandes', which were presumably the booths of the local merchants and craftsmen.

It is unclear how far the settlement pattern at Beech Hill and Causewayend had extended over the course of the seventeenth century; but the number of births recorded in the Register of Baptisms at the end of the century would suggest significant little suburbs. Beech Hill was to remain the site for open-air courts until the building of the Steeple in the late eighteenth century (*see* p 30). There was also settlement in Lay Lyes, Meadow Lyes and Long Leis, Dykehead, Bogside (presumably in the area of present Bogside Road) **I** and 'the boat', which was probably near the present Boatlands **J**.

There are varying local traditions as to the age of Cumberland Barracks **K** *&* **figure 11** in Calton Street (*see* p 28); one view holds that it was in existence in the seventeenth century at the time of the Covenanting wars; another that it was constructed in the early eighteenth century, as a base for anti-Jacobite campaigns. Whatever its origins, Cumberland Barracks was fully functional by the time of the 'Forty–Five campaign.

Other standing buildings are also reminders of Coupar's past (*see* pp 59–63). The Masonic Hall **L** in Gray Street, once used partly as a school, is a fine example of quality building. A number of eighteenth-century houses, or remnants of them, indicate that Coupar was a modestly wealthy, small country town (*see* p 30). 20 Commercial Street **E**, and other properties in Hay Street and Calton Street (*see* p 60) are fine examples of more modest dwellings, while Beech Hill House **A** and the Union Bank Buildings **O** reflect eighteenth-century architecture with nineteenth-century additions.

Many other changes were to be made to the townscape. New access roads—George Street to the west leading to Perth and Union Street to the east of The Cross **figure 15**—relieved some of the congestion in the old main thoroughfare, Calton Street. Still standing are buildings which give a feel of nineteenth-century Coupar Angus (*see* p 61–3). The Secession Church, built in 1826, while somewhat dilapidated in appearance, now functions as the YWCA **P**. A number of nineteenth-century private dwelling houses still stand in Union Street, Calton Street, The Cross, George Square and George Street (*see* pp 61–3). Larger quality buildings survive also, such as Princeland on Blairgowrie Road **Q** and Gartloch Bank on Bogside Road **R** (*see* p 63). In 1887, the Town Hall **D** *&* **figure 20**, a symbol of civic pride, was built at a cost of £4,000, to celebrate Queen Victoria's jubilee.

history

---

archaeology

through to the Middle Bronze Age. It is likely that other burials and traces of other prehistoric activities may lie nearby.

previous archaeological work and chance finds

Beech Hill House NO 220 404 **A, T**

ring-ditch, cists, stone cairn

The renovation of a building initially necessitated the disturbance, and subsequent levelling, of the fluvio-glacial ridge on which the monument stood. An assessment trench dug in May 1989 was followed in June–July 1989 by the complete excavation of the cairn **figure 5**.

ring-ditch

The V-shaped ring-ditch had an average width of 0.5 m and an average depth of 0.6 m. The ditch enclosed an area 8.5 m in diameter, containing patches of old ground surface. Several post pipes were identified in the northern section of the ditch. Sherds of Late Neolithic Grooved Ware were recovered from deposits immediately outside the ring ditch.

archaeology

cist 1
This was located outside the ring-ditch on its south-west side. It consisted of a deep pit, its long axis aligned NW–SE, containing a large quantity of cremated bone, sealed by a capstone and large boulders.

cist 2
This was located west of the ring-ditch and was structurally identical to cist 1. Its long axis was aligned N–S. It also contained a large quantity of cremated bone.

cist 3
This was located within the ring-ditch, in an area of recent disturbance. Its long axis was aligned NW–SE. It consisted of a substantial, boulder-lined pit, the capstone of which was missing, and contained a food vessel.

cist 4
This was located near the centre of the ring-ditch enclosure. It had an E–W long axis. Its southern part had suffered recent disturbance and the capstone was missing. It contained a food vessel.

cist 5
This cist cut the ring-ditch. It consisted of a deep pit, with an E–W long axis. It was constructed of fine sandstone side slabs, covered with a massive capstone, and was sealed by boulders. It contained an inhumation, accompanied by a food vessel.

cairn
Twelve kerb stones remain *in situ* on the N and NE periphery, where they overlie the fill of the ring-ditch and, in places, the old ground surface. Elsewhere, the kerb has been removed by recent disturbance. Its estimated diameter was *c* 8.5 m. The surviving cairn material within the kerb consisted of fist-sized water-rounded stones. The deposit was severely disturbed by root action and had been extensively robbed. The original height of the cairn could not be determined.

The Beech Hill cairn had probably been a focus of activity over a long period of time. Two cists (3 and 4) were built before it was raised; one of them cut an earlier pit which was possibly another grave. Both these cists, and the pit, lay within the area enclosed by the ring-ditch. The fill of this ditch, however, suggested that it had never been an open feature and may have held upright timbers. The ditch had been cut through an earlier pit on the SE, and was itself cut by cist 5. The cairn was set concentrically within the ring-ditch, but the stratigraphic relationship between the two could not be demonstrated conclusively.

The radiocarbon dates from the site could not be relied upon to clarify the sequence of events, but the grave goods show that this cemetery was certainly in use by the beginning of the second millennium BC. Some of the artefacts found beneath the cairn, which included sherds of Late Neolithic Grooved Ware, are thought to derive from manure spreading at an earlier date. *DES* (1989), 63–4; Stevenson (1995), 197–236.

finds assemblage **figure 6**
The finds from the Beech Hill House cairn have been donated to Perth Museum and Art Gallery. *DES* (1993), 100; Stevenson (1995), 197–236.

Beech Hill

cist NO 221 404 **Y**
A stone cist containing human bone was found *c* 1862 in the field a little to the east of the Beech Hill cairn. (NMRS, NO24 SW9).

figure 22
Carved stone head,
Perth Museum
and Art Gallery

archaeology

flint arrowhead NO 219 403 **X**
A barbed and tanged grey flint arrowhead was found on the surface of a field at Beech Hill. The arrowhead is in the possession of the finder. *DES* (1985), 53.

Princeland NO 222 404 **W**

cists
A number of stone 'coffins' containing human bones were found *c* 1899/1900, reportedly rudely fashioned from slabs of local red sandstone. *Scottish Antiquary* (1899), 183.

Beech Hill Place NO 220 403 **N**

Celtic carved stone head **figure 22**
A Celtic head was found in the garden of a house in Beech Hill Place, Coupar Angus, in 1989. The oval head is smoothly finished, with a pedestal-like neck and a flat base allowing the head to stand upright. The face has incised lentoid eyes without pupils, incised curving eyebrows, a large protruding nose starting from the lower forehead, a possible moustache, a straight expressionless incised mouth and small ears in slight relief, hollowed in the centre. The flat crown of the head bears tool-marks, and below the chin are incised two strands of a possible collar or neck fastening. *DES* (1992), 76.

Coupar Angus

bronze pin NO 22 40
A bronze, ring-headed pin was recovered in this approximate area, and is now in private possession. Childe (1935), 234.

stone lamp NO 21 40
A sandstone lamp was found in the neighbourhood of Coupar Angus, and is now located in the National Museums of Scotland. *PSAS* (1898), 239.

the archaeological potential of Coupar Angus a summary **figure 26**

On present evidence, it appears that the overall potential for the survival of archaeological deposits within the medieval core of Coupar Angus is limited. The archaeological potential for surviving evidence of the precincts of the Cistercian monastery is, however, high. Routine monitoring and excavations in many other Scottish burghs, especially Perth and Aberdeen but also in some smaller towns, have demonstrated that medieval and later archaeological remains often survive beneath the modern town. The site of any proposed ground disturbance or development along the main street frontages in the historic section of Coupar Angus, therefore, must be accorded a high archaeological priority, and arrangements made for the site to be assessed, monitored and, if necessary, excavated in advance of any development scheme. Similarly, any proposed ground disturbance of the surviving streets and wynds themselves (for instance, for essential repairs, access to services, or environmental improvements) should also be monitored routinely, because the remains of important features of the medieval townscape may be sealed beneath them—the market cross, tolbooth, tron and wells—of which no archaeological evidence has yet been found.

To date, there have been limited opportunities for archaeological investigation in Coupar Angus, and the few done so far have been biased towards the abbey and its environs. Of necessity, this assessment of the archaeological potential has been made with relatively little evidence from archaeological work in the town. Thus, the conclusions and recommendations expressed here should be regarded as provisional. This survey will require periodic review in the light of results from any future campaigns of archaeological fieldwork (assessment, monitoring and excavation), and from other sub-surface investigations.

It is important to stress that the survey was limited to the core of historic (medieval) Coupar Angus. There is a recognised, though unquantifiable, potential for the discovery of prehistoric and Roman archaeological remains, both within and outwith the confines of the historic burgh (*see* pp 13–16). This potential is *not* considered or shown on **figure 26**.

Finally, the potential for archaeological features and deposits to be preserved both beneath the floors and within the structures of historic standing buildings in Coupar Angus (pp 59–63) must not be forgotten. The archaeological potential of Coupar Angus' standing buildings is *not* shown on **figure 26**, but the potential of individual buildings is considered in the next section.

Turning to the specific areas of Coupar Angus (as identified in this survey), previous work and chance finds have demonstrated the archaeological potential of Areas 1 and 2, with Area 1 clearly the most sensitive to new development.

figure 26 distinguishes between areas of known potential (shaded green) and unknown potential (shaded lighter green). **All green areas should be treated as potentially archaeologically sensitive**. Effectively developed areas (shaded blue) are probably archaeologically sterile.

area 1

The archaeological potential of Area 1 is confined to the abbey precinct, which may extend as far north and east as the Coupar Burn, south to Cothall Track and west to Abbey Gardens and beyond. The sensitivity of this area to development has clearly been demonstrated by the work carried out in the glebe field and by field-walking and chance finds. The main buildings of the abbey and the inner precinct lie to the east of Queen Street/Dundee Road, on the site of, and to the south of, the present parish church. The medieval graveyard lies to the north of the parish church. The only upstanding remnant of the abbey, the probable gatehouse, may define the south side of the inner precinct.

The layout of the outer precinct, however, is largely unknown, and the construction of the A94 relief road produced no archaeological evidence as to whether the northern boundary of the precinct extended as far as the Coupar Burn. A wide range of industrial and agricultural activities was carried out within the precincts of medieval abbeys; their remains may be preserved within gardens, beneath and within the fabric of standing buildings and below modern street levels. Evidence for settlement within the precinct after the Reformation is also likely to be preserved here.

The northern end of Area 1 straddles both the precinct and the burgh. The earliest settlement outwith the abbey is likely to have developed here, outside the main, north gateway into the precinct. The frontages and burgage plots of George Street/Union Street, particularly around The Cross, are, therefore, potentially the earliest in the burgh.

area 2

Much of the eastern, western and northern parts of Area 2 are outwith the historic (medieval) core of the town, and comprise modern residential housing.

The historic core of the town has largely escaped modern development and, as a result, there has been little opportunity for any archaeological investigation.

Early settlement seems to have been focused around the main gateway into the abbey precinct, and to have clustered along the main routes into town. The most sensitive areas are likely to be centred around The Cross, George Square, Gray Street and Commercial Street. The lower stretches of the streets that continue northwards up towards Beech Hill should also be seen as archaeologically sensitive: Hay Street, Calton Street and Causewayend.

Finally, the high potential for further prehistoric remains on Beech Hill must always be borne in mind.

historic buildings

pp 59–63

historic buildings and their archaeological potential

A number of historic buildings still stand, either in part or in whole. These offer clues to Coupar's varied and rich past.

The most important buildings to have stood here were those that comprised the *Cistercian abbey complex*. Little of this historic religious house now remains. To the south of the present parish church, on the Dundee road, are the ruins of what is thought to have been part of one of the entrances or gateways into the precinct. This red sandstone, round, barrel-vaulted pend arch is the sole hint of the splendour of the medieval Cistercian house **figure 23**. From the late sixteenth century, the abbey buildings proved a useful quarry; throughout the town many standing buildings offer evidence of being built from abbey stone.

A little nearer the centre of the town, on the other side of the road, is the *Steeple* **figures 14 & 17.R**. This six-storeyed, red rubble tower with slate roof, clock and weather vane was built by public subscription in 1762. Its heavily barred windows attest to its former use as the town prison. According to local tradition, the tenants of the house immediately to the north, which was partially used as a school, were responsible for feeding the prisoners. Food was passed through the ground floor window of the Steeple, which is, to this day, still accessed from the garden of this neighbouring house. The Steeple was built on the site of

figure 23
Cistercian arch.
Photograph c 1980

figure 24
North-east corner of The Cross in the 1950s

the former High Court of Justiciary, the remains of which may lie buried beneath the present floor levels of the building.

Other eighteenth-century buildings in the town are reminders of Coupar's past. At the north-east corner of *The Cross* **figure 19.U** may be seen an example of two-storeyed vernacular domestic architecture, with shop premises at the ground floor level, now called 'The Corner Shop' **figure 24**. The ogee-roofed corner bay feature is an early twentieth-century addition. In nearby Gray Street, the *Masonic Buildings* **figure 19.L** (St John Operative, No 105), once a school, is an attractive group. The west part is symmetrical, with three round-headed windows at the first floor still retaining their original glazing; the east is two-windowed, with a flat-arch pend, now partially infilled with wooden panelling. On the corner of Gray Street, *20 Commercial Street* **figure 19.E** is also of late eighteenth-century construction. A two-storeyed rubble building, now covered with cement work, it has an interesting Venetian window angle feature at first-floor level.

2 Hay Street is a fine example of modest late Georgian domestic architecture. Well preserved, with architrave with convex frieze and cornice to the door, it was probably built around 1790. The upper windows of this two-storeyed house are modern replacements, but retain the former style of six panes over six. *1 Calton Street* and *11 Calton Street* are typical two-storeyed plain fronted houses. Further along the road, *Aviemore, Calton Street,* also late eighteenth century in date, displays a porch of a common type in this region—five-sided with windows in each of the four outer sides and main door in the central panel.

Buildings situated near the core of the medieval burgh, particularly around *The Cross,* were almost certainly constructed on the site of, or directly over, earlier buildings, a sequence going back to the medieval period and continuing up to the present day. Although there has been no opportunity to examine any of the street frontages in Coupar Angus, evidence of medieval structures in the form of post-holes and floor surfaces may be expected, sealed beneath eighteenth- or nineteenth-century standing buildings such as '*The Corner Shop' (The Cross)* **figure 24**, *20 Commercial Street* **figure 19.E** and the *Royal Hotel (The Cross)* **figures 12 & 17.P**. Within these and other standing buildings in the medieval core of the town, the remains of floor surfaces and other features associated with earlier phases of occupation may be preserved, sealed beneath the modern floor levels.

In other towns, recent excavations have revealed street frontages as the most promising for preservation of archaeological deposits, in spite of the problem of cellarage which may remove earlier evidence. Excavations in Perth, Dunfermline and Arbroath, for example, have also shown that the width and alignment of the main streets in the burgh have changed over the centuries. Earlier cobbled street surfaces and contemporary buildings may therefore be preserved up to three or four metres behind the line of the modern street frontage.

Originally a relatively simple two-storeyed eighteenth-century house, *Beech Hill House* **figure 19.A**, Beech Hill Road had a large bow-fronted T-plan wing added to it early in the nineteenth century. The *Union Bank Buildings* **figure 19.O** and *Bank House*, Calton Street are also examples of eighteenth-century architecture, with a later, nineteenth-century addition. The west part is approximately symmetrical with a centre chimney gablet and Venetian window motif; the east, bow-fronted wing was added later. Calton Street was the main thoroughfare east-west before the arrival of turnpike roads and it was appropriate that an important bank building should have a prestigious main street setting. *7 Gray Street* is also a former bank office, with a centre first-floor Ionic Venetian window and pediment still a reminder of its status and function within the community.

Cumberland Barracks **figures 11 & 19.K**, *2 Calton Street*, named after the duke of Cumberland who led the government forces against the supporters of Prince Charles Edward Stuart, is a significant building in the town. A reminder of more troubled times, it was built in the seventeenth or eighteenth century. Coupar Angus stood at the south end of two roads constructed in the eighteenth century for rapid movement of forces and efficient supplying of remote garrisons. The principal route led via Blairgowrie and Braemar to Fort George on the Moray Firth; Coupar was probably for many men their last stay in the Lowlands. The east wing, which was formerly crowstepped, is the earliest portion of the building; it was extended into a three-storeyed L-plan structure, with a square staircase in the re-entrant angle.

Buildings which have more than one phase of construction may have earlier structural features sealed within the fabric itself, hidden by later additions. Cumberland Barracks, having seen two phases of construction in its history, may have structural elements of the earlier phase sealed within the later fabric, for example behind blocked up doorways.

Coupar was also host to more peaceable visitors. An eighteenth-century hostelry, still standing, is the *Strathmore Hotel* **figures 13 & 17.T**. Formerly known as The White House and the White Horse Inn, it is a two-storeyed building with attics and five-windowed elevation. The entrance porch of tree trunks bearing the weight of the roof was popular in the nineteenth century and may be a later addition. Originally the stables for the horses which drew the travellers' carriages were situated at the rear of the building. A few remnants of these and tethering rings remain to be seen.

On the south-west corner of *The Cross* stands the *Royal Hotel* **figures 12 & 17.P**, once called the Defiance Inn. Its first name was taken from that of the stage coach, which stopped here on its daily journey to and from Edinburgh and Aberdeen. A three-storeyed building with attics (additions were made to it in the nineteenth century), to its west side still stands the nineteenth-century, two-storeyed Assembly Room section, with its ground-floor shops, pend arch and tall first floor. The Defiance Inn was re-named the Royal Hotel after 1844, when Queen Victoria and Prince Albert spent the night there.

In the mid nineteenth century Coupar became a staging post for passengers using a newer form of transport—the railway. A far-sighted banker, David Anderson, realised the potential of railway traffic and built the Railway Hotel, now called the *Red House Hotel* **figure 17.Z**. The original hotel had six rooms to let, a dining room and a bar. Now much altered and extended, it continues to function as a stopping post for travellers, but the passenger railway disappeared in 1967 as a result of Dr Beeching's radical measures, and all trains ceased to pass through Coupar in 1982.

Other nineteenth-century buildings attest to Coupar's role as a modest, but important small centre of industry. A few remnants of the old *tannery* **figure 17.T** remain north of Precinct Street; the *mill* **figure 17.L** which stood on the south bank of Coupar Burn, to the north of Thorn Alley has been re-developed; no structural remains are left of the old timber market; and the railway that serviced these industries has also disappeared **figure 25**. Some of the buildings still standing, however, give insights into nineteenth-century Coupar Angus.

A new *parish church* **figure 17.A** was erected to a design of John Carver of Kinloch in 1859–60. Red rubble with white sandstone dressings, it has a southerly porch and a north-west tower with a small slated spire. Its west window and hammerbeam roof are impressive. A number of relics from previous churches on the site were incorporated: the font is composed of a nave pier; a panel of low relief figures—the Weepers—has been

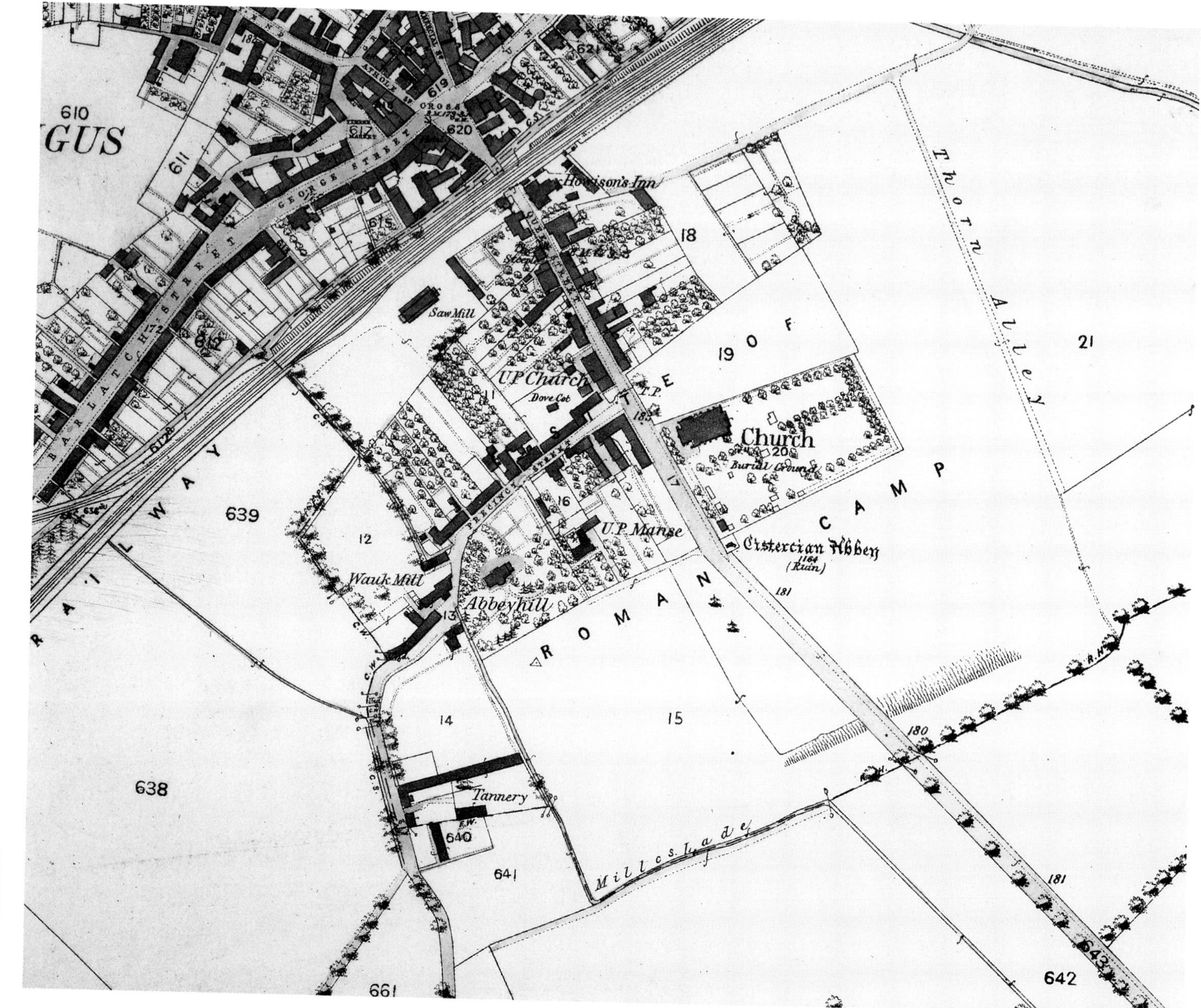

figure 25
25 inch Ordnance Survey map of Coupar Angus 1860

retained; and the tomb effigy of Sir Thomas Hay, third constable of Scotland, lies in the interior of the church. In the graveyard outside, other members of the Hay family are buried, alongside many of the humbler Coupar people who died in the eighteenth and nineteenth centuries. In the graveyard is another interesting structure, the circular *watch-tower*, built in the 1820s of abbey stone. Its purpose was to provide shelter for the watchmen who were on the look-out for grave-robbers.

The parish church, graveyard and the standing remains of the gatehouse all lie within the scheduled area, and development here is unlikely. Environmental improvements and the insertion of new services, both within the standing building and in the graveyard area are likely, however and they will certainly disturb archaeological remains.

Over the last two centuries, improvements inside the church and in the graveyard, both of which had been established over the main abbey complex, have brought to light a number of important discoveries. In the late eighteenth century, groundworks at the west end of the church revealed more than twelve stone coffins, whilst in 1887 two more stone coffins and a possible long cist were found in the burial-ground. Any further groundworks may expose earlier phases of the present parish church, built in 1859–60, as well as traces of the earlier abbey church. Evidence of a pre-abbey church or settlement here is also a possibility.

Another church, the Secession Church, was built in 1826, set back from Union Street. Now the *YWCA* **figure 19.P**, it still retains many of its original features: piended roof, ashlar façade, with two tall round-headed windows, and its original glazing. Along the street, *Dalblair*, Union Street is the former Free Church Manse, erected in 1845. An attractive dwelling, it is two-storeyed with an attic and architrave to its door. Across the road, *Kyldon House*, a *c* 1835 dwelling house with three-windowed elevation, architrave with square lugs to the door and bayed windows, is indicative of the prosperity of some members of the Coupar community; as is *Millburn*, George Street, a two-storeyed house with architrave and conclave spray to its door and six over six sash windows.

Several other examples of local, nineteenth-century architecture still stand. At the *south-east corner of The Cross*, for example, a three-storeyed building with dormer heads at the top floor now houses W Davidson and Sons, Chemists on the ground floor. At *3 Commercial Street*, a much altered early nineteenth-century building retains some of its early attractiveness. It has a centre chimney gablet and R-doric column doorway. Now a grocery/ snack food takeaway, large windows have been placed on each side of the doorway and replacement windows have been inserted in the upper floor. A group of buildings at *George Square* and *2 Causewayend* is indicative of period architecture. Built around 1871, they have the appearance of having incorporated earlier structures. Two-storeyed rubble domestic architecture, there is an interesting chamfered corner feature at Causewayend and a fore-stair at the obtuse angled block at the west end. Nearby, *3 Causewayend* is a typical three-windowed rubble, vernacular domestic building.

A few examples of larger, quality buildings survive. *Princeland* **figure 19.Q**, Blairgowrie Road was originally a two-storey building with basement in a U-plan, with an entrance in the recess. It has a screen wall with a segmental arch and a pyramid-roofed stable. An entrance hall with bathroom over was added at the turn of the century. *Gartloch Bank* **figure 19.R** on Bogside Road is a very attractive single-storey red ashlar house. The older, three-bay centre section was built in the early nineteenth century and the bays added a little later. A rect-angular ice-house and wine cellar in a bank at the rear were part of the original features. *Enverdale House* **figure 17.O** was built in 1875 by the McFarlanes. Local industrialists, they owned the Strathmore Linen Works, which manufactured for home and abroad. Their quality building has now been extended and converted into a hotel. The work premises were equally well designed and constructed, but like many other remnants of Coupar's industrial past, these were demolished, in 1994.

The *Town Hall* **figures 19.D & 20** is perhaps the symbol of Coupar's nineteenth-century civic pride. Built in 1887, at a cost of £4,000, it was erected to mark Queen Victoria's jubilee. Retaining most of its former grandeur, it now hosts various local functions, acts as meeting place for the community council and houses the local library and the robes of the last provost of Coupar Angus.

suggested avenues for further work

pp 65–7

historical objectives for further research

The rental records and charters of Coupar Angus Abbey have proved important documentary sources for an understanding of the workings of Coupar Abbey and an imprecise overview of its lay-out; they have also given an insight into settlement clustered near the abbey gates. Some questions, however, have not been answered by the documentary data, and may never be. It would appear that there was settlement in the Coupar area immediately prior to the founding of the Cistercian abbey, but nothing is known of it. The question has been raised in the text of whether the Cistercians first came to Coupar Angus or possibly settled elsewhere in their first years, perhaps north of the Isla. This has been left open and it should be considered in more depth. Neither is the precise lay-out of the abbey and its precincts fully clarified. Given that the archaeological potential for survival of deposits associated with the abbey is high, there may here be a rare opportunity of gaining a fuller understanding of a Cistercian complex by a combination of historical and archaeological research and excavation.

The documentary resource has been more revealing for post-Reformation times. There are, however, a number of avenues that might merit further attention. These may give a clearer picture of urban life and the pattern of settlement at the time of the late medieval

archaeological objectives for the future

Preparation of the Coupar Angus burgh survey has highlighted a number of directions for future archaeological work. These can be broadly divided into management objectives, priorities for future fieldwork and other areas which merit further research. Any such list cannot be exhaustive, but it should cover the main areas of concern in the foreseeable future.

management objectives

1. Wherever possible, it is important to monitor the impact of any development (in its broadest sense) on the potential archaeological resource (the **green** areas on **figure 26**). This will require the routine provision of site-specific desk-based assessments, through to watching briefs, trial excavations and, where necessary, controlled excavation, post-excavation analysis and publication. Over time, the cumulative results will 'calibrate' this assessment of the archaeological potential of the burgh, providing evidence about the burgh's origins, and its physical, economic and social development through the centuries.

2. Developments should similarly be monitored to shed more light on the prehistory of Coupar Angus and on its function in the Roman sphere of influence.

3. The degree and nature of cellarage along the main streets were not systematically examined during the preparation of this report. More accurate information would be most useful to managers/curators of the archaeological resource in assessing the archaeological potential of these and other main street frontages in the burgh.

4. Engineers' boreholes offer a convenient glimpse of the depth and nature of sub-surface deposits, man-made or not, ancient and modern. It would be useful if the results obtained from engineers' boreholes in and around the core of the historic burgh could be gradually collected and collated. Borehole results, especially those in the hands of private contractors, have proved difficult to access, and it might be worth considering mechanisms by which such information could more easily (and preferably routinely) be made available to managers/curators of the archaeological resource.

township and at its elevation into a burgh in 1607. The site of the northern gate of the abbey where the market cross stood is not known precisely, but is important for a clear understanding of the medieval topography of the township. It is known that the town colonised the erstwhile abbey precincts in the seventeenth century, but how rapidly the Cistercian fabric declined and in what manner the suburb of 'Precinct' grew up is not totally clear.

A number of landed families, such as the earls of Atholl and Argyll, became involved in events pertaining to Coupar Angus. Their family papers, such as those of the Campbell family, the earls of Argyll (the Breadalbane Muniments) may prove a useful resource; as may other Atholl and Argyll documentation deposited in SRO, such as NRAS, 234 (Atholl), GD 237 (Atholl), NRAS 396/40 (Argyll) and NRAS 1209 (Argyll). The Airlie Muniments have also been used in this Survey, but a closer examination of the material would be recommended.

James Elphinstone, created Lord Coupar and superior of the newly erected Coupar Angus burgh in 1607, died in 1669. His heir was his nephew John, third Baron Balmerino. The last Lord Balmerino, Arthur, was beheaded for his part in the Jacobite rising of 1745. Ten years later, his confiscated estates were redeemed by his nephew James, seventh earl of Moray. It is, therefore, possible that some of the records of the Elphinstone and

history

archaeology

5 Opportunities should continue to be taken to increase public awareness of the potential archaeological interest of Coupar Angus, both generally and within and beneath historic standing buildings.

6 Periodic review and updating of this survey would be desirable, to take account of the results of any future archaeological work and of the comprehensive collection and collation of other types of sub-surface investigations, including engineers' bore holes, and systematic survey of cellarage on the main street frontages. In particular, the colour-coded map **figure 26** should be revised and re-issued at regular intervals.

priorities for future fieldwork

Although some archaeological work has been undertaken in Coupar Angus, the priorities for future archaeological fieldwork remain fairly rudimentary. The following priorities, however, should be borne in mind during preparations of future project designs.

1 Ascertain the date and nature of the earliest settlement in Coupar Angus, and confirm that settlement existed prior to the establishment of the Cistercian monastery.

2 Define the limits of the abbey precinct and the nature of its boundaries and gateways; Thorn Alley, for example, may represent the upstanding remains of the precinct's eastern boundary, or, as has been suggested, the defences of an earlier Roman camp. Alternatively, the precinct may have extended as far as the Coupar Burn on both the east and north sides of the precinct.

3 Locate the main complex of abbey buildings—church, cloisters, guest accommodation, brewhouses, bakehouses and granaries, for example—and the boundary of the inner precinct within which they stood.

Balmerino families may be subsumed in the Moray Muniments at Darnaway Castle. Although the Inventory of the Moray Muniments has been used for this Survey, the collection itself would merit close attention.

Five sixteenth- and seventeenth-century protocol books, which it was hoped would contain Coupar material, were studied with no reward. A further search through these and the numerous protocol books originating from the wider Coupar Angus area, now deposited in SRO, may result in a few more clues about the seventeenth-century town.

A clearer picture may be gained of the modern town. Lack of time, however, prevented a full use of such sources as the nineteenth-century minute book of the town committee, which is extant for the years 1826–52. The records of the Masonic Lodge St John Operative No 105, if accessible, might hold pertinent information. Another very useful resource, which could not be used to the full, was local knowledge. Further talks with the people of Coupar might, for example, have shed light on why Causewayend was so named, and whether there was a second ford at the end of it, at Butterybank **figure 19**. A number of old properties have wells in their gardens. Most of these have been infilled in recent decades for security, with no written record of their existence. There was no time to undertake a survey of many such recently disappeared features, which are, as yet, alive in the memories of the Coupar people.

history

archaeology

4 Determine the layout of the outer precinct and, in particular, the range and nature of activities undertaken there: industrial (mills, kilns, smithies and tanneries) and cultivation or food production (gardens, orchards, fish-ponds and meadows).

5 Define the limits of the medieval burgh and the character and date of any burgh boundaries.

6 Locate important features of the medieval townscape—the tolbooth, market cross, tron and wells, for example—of which no archaeological evidence has yet been found. The exact location of the north gate into the abbey, which clearly influenced the development of the burgh, is also unknown.

7 Identify any sequence of planning in the layout and expansion of the burgh, and determine any variation in street alignment and width.

8 Assess the nature of the burgage plots in both the burgh and later infill settlement within the abbey precinct.

areas for further archaeological research

1 A reconstruction of the layout, extent and physical setting of the burgh and abbey precinct would be useful for our understanding of the development of the burgh. This would be particularly useful when assessing the impact of future development and in presenting the current state of knowledge.

2 Recent aerial photographic surveys at Coupar Grange have identified a complex of cropmarks associated with this monastic grange. Granges were also established nearby at Aberbothrie, Keithick and Balbrogie. Little is known of the inner workings of these farms in Scotland, and further research here would shed more light on the management and economics of Coupar Angus Abbey.

street names

pp 69–71

Athole Street

Area 2
The Dukes of Atholl donated large areas of land to the abbey, hence the name of the street.

Beech Hill Road

Area 2
Beech Hill, overlooking the town and the River Isla, probably takes its name from the many beech trees that grow nearby. This was also the site of the court and gibbet of the regality before the Steeple was built.

Blairgowrie Road

Area 2
This road was the main route to Blairgowrie.

Bogside Road

Area 2
Lying at the foot of Beech Hill, this area was traditionally marshy ground.

Butterybank

Area 2
Formerly known as Buttress bank, Butterybank was situated on the old military road. The crossing over the River Isla was reputedly nearby.

Campbell Street

Area 2
Donald Campbell was the last abbot of Coupar Angus Abbey and held office between 1526 and 1562.

Candlehouse Lane

Area 1
This lane was named after a candle factory which was situated here. The building still stands and stones from the abbey can be seen in its fabric. The abbey mill also stood nearby, drawing water from the Coupar Burn.

Calton Street

Area 2
A jail was situated here, opposite Cumberland Barracks. The jail may have been named after Calton Hill, Edinburgh, where offenders were hanged.

Causewayend

Area 2
Some claim that this means the way to the causey. The ford across the Isla, however, was possibly further east of Bendochy church. The name may derive from 'causey', meaning cobbled.

Coach Road

Area 2
Coach Road connects Causewayend with Bogside Road. A tradition records that heavier vehicles used to take this road to avoid the marshier land.

Commercial Street

Area 2
This was once one of the busiest commercial areas of town and was where a number of shops and businesses were located. Many of these have been demolished and the area is now used as a car park.

Cothall Track

Area 1
This track or right of way was named after the Victorian villa which stands nearby.

The Cross	*Areas 1 & 2* Named after the market cross which stood here.
Church Place	*Area 2* Church Place was named after the Congregational church which stood here.
Cuddy's Wynd	*Area 2* Heavy horses were led from Trades Lane across busy George Street and down Cuddy's Wynd to water at the Coupar Burn.
Dalrymple Place	*Area 2* This close was named after the owner. An unusual stairwell, known locally as a 'rump', can be seen here; it allowed access for horses to the first floor of what was a stable-block. It has since been renovated as an office.
Dundee Road	*Area 1* This is the main road to Dundee and passes through the erstwhile medieval abbey precinct.
Forfar Road	*Area 2* This was the main road to Forfar.
George Square	*Area 2* George Square was named after the monarch, George III.
George Street	*Areas 1 & 2* George Street was also named after George III.
Gray Street	*Area 2* This street was named after T B Gray, a local councillor.
Hay Street	*Area 2* The Hays of Errol were one of the abbey's largest benefactors. Many of the family are buried in the parish kirkyard.
High Street	*Area 1* In most medieval towns, the High Street is the main thoroughfare and often the longest street. The High Street in Coupar Angus is recognised as the shortest High Street in Britain.
Hill Street	*Area 2* This street probably takes its name from the hill that slopes down southwards from Beech Hill.
King's Road	*Area 2* King's Road was named after the Prince Regent, later George IV.
Perth Road	*Area 2* This is the main road to Perth and is essentially a continuation of George Street.
Pleasance Road	*Area 1* This road leads to Pleasance Farm from Precinct Street.

Precinct Street

Area 1
This street lies within the boundary, or precinct, of the medieval abbey.

Princes Croft

Area 2
Princes Croft was named after the Prince Regent, later George IV.

Queen Street

Area 1
Queen Victoria passed through Coupar Angus en route to Balmoral, staying at the Defiance Inn (the Royal Hotel) and this street was named after her, in celebration of the event.

School Road

Area 2
The school was situated here.

St Catherine's Lane

Area 2
This street was named after the saint.

Thorn Alley

Area 1
Thorn Alley, a right of way, comprises a raised, grassy linear mound and may mark a Roman camp. Tradition also claims it to delineate the eastern boundary of the abbey precinct, but this was possibly further east, on the bank of the Coupar Burn.

Trades Lane

Area 2
Trades Lane was once the home to a number of skilled artisans, mainly blacksmiths, who serviced the stables which stood at the end of this lane.

Union Street

Areas 1 & 2
This is now the main thoroughfare in the town. The name 'Union' is thought to derive from the many roads that meet here, although in many other towns this name is thought to refer to the parliamentary union of 1707.

Victoria Street

Area 2
This street was named after Queen Victoria who passed through Coupar Angus en route to Balmoral. On an overnight stop, she stayed in the Defiance Inn, later re-named the Royal Hotel in her honour.

glossary

pp 73–5

glossary

artefacts	Objects made by human workmanship.
backlands	The area to the rear of the burgage plot behind the dwelling house on the frontage. Originally intended for growing produce and keeping animals; site of wells and midden heaps. Eventually housed working premises of craftsmen and poorer members of burgh society.
bailies	Burgh officers who performed routine administration.
boundaries	*see* burgage plot
burgage plot	A division of land, often of regular size, having been measured out by liners, allocated to a burgess. Once built on, it contained the burgage house on the frontage (*see* frontage) and a backland (*see* backland). In time, with pressure for space, the plots were often subdivided—repletion. Plots were bounded by ditches, wattle fences or stone walls.
burgess	Person who enjoys the privileges and responsibilities of the freedom of the burgh.
cairn	Mound of stones, often covering Bronze Age burials.
chapter house	A building where members of a monastic order met.
cists	Stone-lined graves.
cloisters	Covered walkway around a courtyard.
close	*see* vennel
cordiners	Leather workers.
craft	Trade.
cross slab	Sculptured stone bearing a cross in relief.
documentary sources	Written evidence, primary sources being the original documents.
drumlin	Mound formed by glacial activity.
façade	Finished face of a building.
Flavian	A period in Roman history, dating to the late first century AD.
fluvioglacial	Combined action of water and ice.
food vessel	A distinctive type of pottery dating to the Bronze Age, often found accompanying burials.
frontage	Front part of burgage plot nearest the street, on which the dwelling was usually built.

gap sites	Burgage plots not built up or 'biggit'; in a modern context, undeveloped space between two buildings.
guild	Organisation or fraternity for mutual support, whether economic, religious or social.
hinterland	Rural area around a burgh, to which the burgh looked for economic and agricultural support; hinterland likewise dependent on burgh market.
hoard	A collection of material deposited in the ground, often buried for safe-keeping but never recovered.
igneous rock	Rock produced by volcanic agency.
Improvement	Period beginning in the eighteenth century when land was improved and enclosed.
indwellers	Unprivileged, non-burgess dwellers in a town.
infilled	Open area that has later been developed.
inhumation	An uncremated human burial.
in situ	An archaeological term describing layers of soil or features undisturbed by later activity.
metamorphic	Rock that has undergone transformation by natural agencies.
merk	13s 4d, two-thirds of £ Scots.
midden	Rubbish heaps consisting of mainly food debris and other waste products, often found in the backlands of medieval properties.
precinct	Area enclosed within boundaries of abbey.
prehistory	Period of human history before the advent of writing.
radiocarbon	Technique used in archaeology to date organic materials.
refectory	Eating room in monastery.
repletion	*see* burgage plot
rig	*see* burgage plot
sherd	Fragment of pottery.
souterrain	Stone-built underground passage dating from between the late first millennium BC and the early first millennium AD.
tectonic movements	Displacements in the earth's crust.
temporary camp	Often called marching camps, these were constructed for temporary accommodation by the Roman army on military campaigns.

terracing	Cutting into a slope to level the ground surface.
toft	*see* burgage plot
tolbooth	The most important secular building; meeting place of burgh council; collection post for market tolls; often housed town gaol.
tolls	Payments for use of burgh market.
townhouse	Principal modern civic building.
tron	Public weigh-beam.
urban nucleus	Original site(s) from which town developed.
vennel	Alley; narrow lane.
£	£ Scots.

bibliography

pp 77–9

City of Dundee Archive and Record Centre
CC1, no 17.

Scottish Record Office
CH2/395/1, Coupar Angus Kirk Session Records, 1682–1703.
CH2/395/2, Coupar Angus Kirk Session Records, 1703–24, which includes the Register of Disciplinary Proceedings of the Church Session of Coupar, together with a Monthly and Annual Account of the Poor's Money.
CH2/395/3, Coupar Angus Kirk Session Records, 1724–6.
CH2/395/4, Coupar Angus Kirk Session Records, 1726–47.
E69/19/2 Hearth Tax, Presbyteries of Perth and Dunkeld.
GD 16/36/7 Airlie Muniments.
GD 16/36/25 Minute Book of the Inhibitions, Hornings *etc*, Registered in the Particular Register of the Regality of Coupar Angus, 1731–46.
GD 16/36/29 Head Court Roll of the Lordship and Regality of Coupar Angus.
GD 16/41/108, Airlie Muniments.
Handlist of documents of Alexander II, SRO open shelf.
National Register of Archives (Scotland) 217, Inventory of the Moray Muniments, vol x, box no 32.
NP1/16 Protocol book of Duncan Gray, 1554–1572.
NP1/43 Protocol book of R Brown, 1584–1607.
NP1/72 Protocol book of A Keltie, 1620–1631.
NP1/86 Protocol book of Patrick Gourlaws, 1637–64.
NP1/161 Protocol book of William Henderson, writer in Meagre, seventeenth century.
TE5/218 Teind Records.

A K Bell Library, Perth
279/1–4 RNE, Baptismal Records, Coupar Angus.

printed primary sources and reference works

Accounts of the Lord High Treasurer of Scotland, 13 vols, edd T Dickson *et al* (Edinburgh, 1877–).
The Acts of the Parliaments of Scotland, 12 vols, edd T Thomson & C Innes (Edinburgh, 1814–1875).
Calendar of Papal Letters to Scotland of Clement VII of Avignon, 1378–1394, ed C Burns (SHS, 1976).
Calendar of Scottish Supplications to Rome, 1428–32, edd A I Dunlop & I B Cowan (SHS, 1970).
Calendar of State Papers relating to Scotland and Mary Queen of Scots, 1547–1603, 13 vols, edd J Bain *et al* (Edinburgh, 1898–1969), vol x, edd W K Boyd & H W Meikle (Edinburgh, 1936).
Cowan, I B & Easson, D E, *Medieval Religious Houses. Scotland* (London, 1976).
Easson, D E (ed), *Charters of the Abbey of Coupar Angus*, 2 vols (SHS, 1947).
Extracts from the Records of the Burgh of Edinburgh, AD 1557–1571 (SBRS, 1875).
Fraser, W (ed), *The Elphinstone Family Book of the Lords Elphinstone, Balmerino and Coupar*, 2 vols (Edinburgh, 1897).
Hannay, R K (ed), *Rentale Dunkeldense, being Accounts of the Bishopric (AD 1505–1517), with Myln's 'Lives of the bishops' (AD 1483–1517)* (SHS, 1915).
Jocelyn, 'Life of Waltheof', *Acta Sanctorum Bollandi, August*, i.
Kirk, J (ed), *The Books of Assumption of the Thirds of Benefices. Scottish Ecclesiastical Rentals at the Reformation* (Oxford, 1995).
Macfarlane, W, 'Geographical description of severall parishes in Perthshire, 1st of the paroch of Alyth' in *Geographical Collections Relating to Scotland*, ed A Mitchell, 3 vols (SHS, 1906–8).

Maidment, J (ed), *The Spottiswoode Miscellany*, 2 vols (Edinburgh, 1844–5).
The New Statistical Account of Scotland, vol x, *Perthshire* (Edinburgh, 1845).
Pococke, R, *Tours in Scotland 1747, 1750, 1760*, ed D W Kemp (SHS, 1887).
Regesta Regum Scottorum:
vol i *The Acts of Malcolm IV, King of Scots, 1153–1165*, ed G W S Barrow (Edinburgh, 1960).
vol ii *The Acts of William I, King of Scots, 1165–1214*, ed G W S Barrow with W W Scott (Edinburgh, 1971).
vol v *The Acts of Robert I, King of Scots, 1306–1329*, ed A A M Duncan (Edinburgh, 1988).
vol vi *The Acts of David II, King of Scots, 1329–1371*, ed B Webster (Edinburgh, 1982).
The Register of the Great Seal of Scotland (Registrum Magni Sigilli Regum Scotorum), 11 vols, edd J M Thomson *et al* (Edinburgh, 1882–1914).
The Register of the Privy Council of Scotland, edd J H Burton *et al*: first series, 14 vols (Edinburgh, 1877–98), second series, 8 vols (Edinburgh, 1899–1908), third series, 16 vols (Edinburgh 1908–).
The Register of the Privy Seal of Scotland (Registrum Secreti Sigilli Regum Scotorum), 8 vols, edd M Livingston *et al* (Edinburgh 1908–).
Rogers, C (ed), *Rental Book of the Cistercian Abbey of Cupar-Angus with the Breviary of the Register*, 2 vols (Grampian Club, 1879–80).
Roy, W, *Military Antiquities of the Romans in Britain* (London, 1793).
Spalding, J, *The History of the Troubles and Memorable Transactions in Scotland and England from MDCXXIV to MDCXLV (1624–1645)*, 2 vols (Bannatyne Club, 1829).
The Statistical Account of Scotland 1791–9, vol xi, *South and East Perthshire, Kinross-shire*, new edition, edd D J Withrington & I R Grant, (Wakefield, 1976).

secondary sources

Alfonso, I, 'Cistercians and feudalism', *Past and Present*, cxxxiii (1991).
Barclay, G J, Maxwell, G S, Simpson, I A & Davidson, D A, 'The Cleaven Dyke: a Neolithic cursus monument/bank barrow in Tayside Region, Scotland', *Antiquity* vol 69, no 263 (June 1995), 317–26.
Brown, C J & Shipley, B M, *Soil Survey of Scotland: South-East Scotland. Soil and Land Capability for Agriculture* (The Macaulay Institute for Soil Research, Aberdeen, 1982).
Brown, K M, *Bloodfeud in Scotland, 1573–1625* (Edinburgh, 1986).
Coppack, G, 'The excavation of an outer court building, perhaps the wool-house at Fountains Abbey, North Yorkshire', *Medieval Archaeology*, xxx (1986), 46–87.
Courtney, P, 'Excavations in the outer precinct of Tintern Abbey', *Medieval Archaeology*, xxxiii (1989), 99–143.
Darvill, T, *Prehistoric Britain* (London, 1987).
Dilworth, M, 'Monks and ministers after 1560', *Records of the Scottish Church History Society*, xviii (1974).
Dingwall, C H, *Ardler—A Village History. The Planned Railway Village of Washington* (Abertay Historical Society, 1985).
Donkin, R A, *Cistercian Studies in the Geography of England and Wales* (Toronto, 1988).
Edmonds, E, *The Geological Map: an Anatomy of a Landscape* (HMSO, London, 1983).
Franklin, T B, *A History of Scottish Farming* (Edinburgh, 1952).
Groome, F H, *Ordnance Gazetteer of Scotland: A Survey of Scottish Topography*, 6 vols (Edinburgh, 1886).
Hanson, W & Maxwell, G, *Rome's North-West Frontier: The Antonine Wall* (Edinburgh, 1983).
Heron, R, *Scotland Delineated* (Edinburgh, 1975; original published 1799).
Keppie, L, *Scotland's Roman Remains* (Edinburgh, 1986).
King, P, 'Coupar Angus and Cîteaux', *Innes Review*, xxvii (1976).
Laing, M (ed), *Coupar Angus Newsletter* (Coupar Angus, 1994), no 41.
Maxwell, G, *The Romans in Scotland* (Edinburgh, 1989).
Macdonald, J A R, *The History of Blairgowrie* (Blairgowrie, 1899).

McGibbon, T & Ross, D, *The Ecclesiastical Architecture of Scotland*, 3 vols (Edinburgh, 1897).
O'Sullivan, J, 'Abbey, market and cemetery: topographical notes on Coupar Angus in Perthshire, with a description of archaeological excavations on glebe land by the parish church', *PSAS* 125 (1995), 1045–1068.
Perthshire Advertiser, Centenary Number, Special Edition, 1929.
Royal Commission on the Ancient and Historical Monuments of Scotland, *South-East Perth: an Archaeological Landscape* (Edinburgh, 1994).
Sissons, J B, *The Geomorphology of the British Isles: Scotland* (London, 1976).
Stevenson, S, 'The excavation of a kerbed cairn at Beech Hill House, Coupar Angus, Perthshire', *PSAS* 125 (1995), 197–236.
Torrie, E P D, *Medieval Dundee. A Town and its People* (Abertay Historical Society, 1990).
Walker, B & Ritchie, G, *Exploring Scotland's Heritage: Fife and Tayside* (Edinburgh, 1993).
Warden, A J, 'Parish of Coupar Angus', *Angus or Forfarshire—the Land and People* (Edinburgh, 1881).

unpublished secondary sources

Crowley, N, 'An archaeological investigation of a drain in Coupar Angus' (Unpublished typescript, AOC (Scotland) Ltd, 1996).
RCAHMS, National Sites and Monuments Record Cards.
Rees, T & Duffy, A 'Archaeological assessment of the sawmill site, Queen Street, Coupar Angus' (Unpublished typescript, AOC (Scotland) Ltd, 1994).

cartographic sources

'Laich of Angus', by Timothy Pont, *c* 1596.
'Anguss', by Robert Gordon of Straloch, *c* 1630.
'Angusia', in J Blaeu, *Atlas Novus* (Amsterdam, 1654).
'The Shire of Angus', by Robert Edwards, 1678.
'The Mappe of Straithern, Stormont, & Cars of Gaurie, with the rivers Tay and Ern', by John Adair, 1683.
'The Mappe of Straithern, Stormont, & Cars of Gaurie, with the rivers Tay and Ern', by John Adair, 1720.
'A Map of His Majesty's Roads', by R Cooper, 1746.
'The Counties of Perth and Clackmannan', by James Stobie, 1783.
'The County of Forfar, by John Ainslie, 1794.
'The Estate of Kethick, property of the late Right Honourable James Stewart MacKenzie, Lord Privy Seal for Scotland.' Surveyed by James Galloway, 1802, SRO RHP 30618.
'Perthshire and Forfarshire', Ordnance Survey Map, 1820.
'The Southern part of Angusshire', by John Thompson, 1825.
'Scottish Midland Junction Railway, Blairgowrie Branch. Plan of ground taken from the property of E Collins Wood Esq. for this Railway', 1854, SRO RHP 30617.
Ordnance Survey 25 inch to the mile, 1860.
Ordnance Survey 1:10,000 (nd).
Ordnance Survey 1:2,500, sheet nos. 2139, 2140, 2239, 2240 (1995).

index

pp 81–6

general index

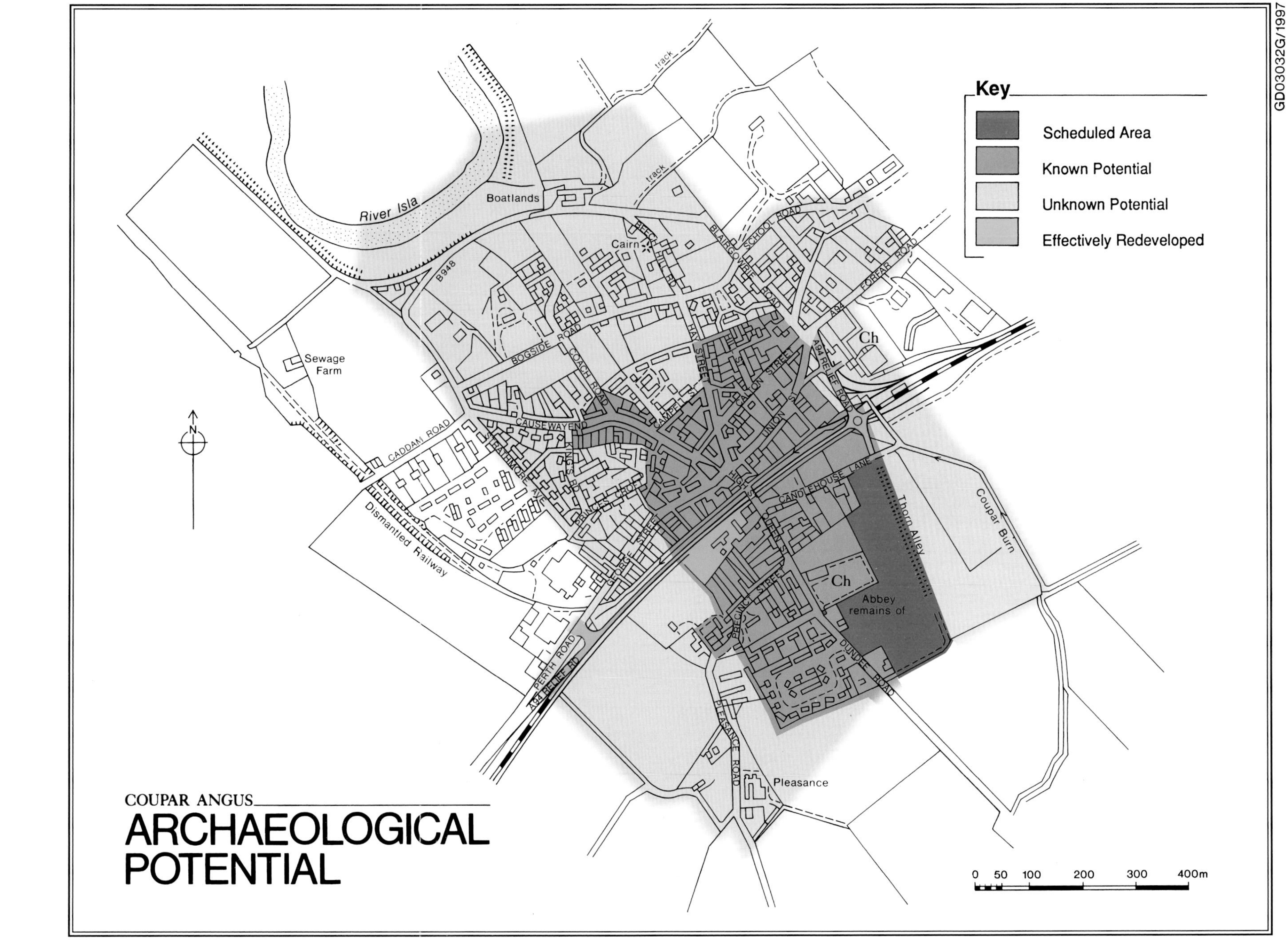

figure 26
The archaeological potential
of Coupar Angus
© Crown Copyright